The Scientific Publication System in Social Science

A Study of the Operation
of Leading Professional Journals
in Psychology, Sociology, and Social Work

Duncan Lindsey

The Scientific
Publication System
in Social Science

 Jossey-Bass Publishers
San Francisco • Washington • London • 1978

THE SCIENTIFIC PUBLICATION SYSTEM IN SOCIAL SCIENCE
*A Study of the Operation of Leading Professional Journals in Psychology,
Sociology, and Social Work*
by Duncan Lindsey

Copyright © 1978 by: Jossey-Bass, Inc., Publishers
433 California Street
San Francisco, California 94104

&

Jossey-Bass Limited
28 Banner Street
London EC1Y 8QE

Library of Congress Catalogue Card Number LC 78-62570

International Standard Book Number ISBN 0-87589-390-2

Manufactured in the United States of America

JACKET DESIGN BY WILLI BAUM

FIRST EDITION

Code 7832

The Jossey-Bass
Social and
Behavioral Science Series

Preface

This book represents an overview and assessment of what is currently known about the character and operations of the scientific publication system in psychology, sociology, and social work. Specifically, it focuses on the system responsible for journal publication and the impact that system has on the nature of dialogue and inquiry in the social and behavioral sciences.

The major motivation for undertaking this study of the journal system arises from a concern that the scientific publication system has been inadequate, not only in providing accurate and meritorious review of the work of practicing scientists, but in the more crucial effort of fostering a spirit of critical questioning about significant issues so essential to the furtherance of human understanding and the growth of knowledge.

A second motivation stems from a belief that potential and even knowledgeable contributors have far too little information about the review process of articles submitted for consideration. What happens to a paper when it arrives at the editorial office of a journal? How long does it currently take to have a paper reviewed? How accurate and fair is the review process?

Who are the people who sit in judgment on the publishability of a paper?

Since journal publication is the primary means of disseminating research findings and contributing to the development of knowledge in a discipline, professionals should understand the process that either accepts or rejects their work. If their articles are not published, scientists are severely hampered in two respects: they lose key opportunities both to share the products of their labors and to allow their performance to be judged by their peers. Without distribution and the attendant assessment of the results of scientific inquiry, professionals may find themselves working in a vacuum. Verbal or written communication with friends and colleagues at a particular institution or within a circle of researchers concerned with a specific problem cannot replace the much broader impact of a published paper. Promotions, career opportunities at other institutions, invitations to undertake special studies, and feedback and criticism from fellow researchers—all so essential to the professional lives of scientists—are inevitably connected with publication, primarily in professional journals.

My first objective in writing this book, then, is to increase the awareness of social scientists of the scientific publication system and its significance to their careers. The findings from my research contain practical information that professionals in psychology, sociology, and social work can use in the process of more effectively reporting their studies. I have attempted to include information to answer the questions posed earlier, if not specifically for all journals, at least generally, so that social scientists can approach journal publication with greater understanding and knowledge.

My second objective is to contribute to the sociology of science by reporting the findings of an empirical study of the scientific publication system. As I have already conveyed, I believe this system is one of the most crucial institutions of science—crucial not only to the scientist's career but also to the development of knowledge. In fact, because the products of this system (scientific papers, books, and their citations) are the key variables in most analyses of the sociology of science, the publication system is the beginning point of any thorough study in this area.

In the spirit of critical theory, I have assessed the current operations of the social science publication system against the background of a clearly identified set of values. As I have identified problems in the system, I have made recommendations for coping with them. My hope is that social and behavioral scientists will become more involved in the effort to improve the scientific publication system, for doing so will improve the health of the scientific community. I offer this book as a guide and impetus to that involvement.

Acknowledgments

While examining these issues, I have had the good fortune to be able to share my emerging analysis with several outstanding scholars and empirical investigators. Howard Becker, Hubert M. Blalock, Jr., Arlene Kaplan Daniels, and Warren Solomon have been most generous with their time and consideration. In addition, correspondence and discussion with Richard Crandall, Diana Crane, Alfred Kahn, Stuart Kirk, Michael Mahoney, James McCartney, Jeffrey Pfeffer, Derek Price, Hyman Rodman, Steven Schinke, William Yoels, and Harriet Zuckerman have made me aware of the complexities and alternative views that serve understanding of the scientific publication system. These colleagues have forced reconsideration of a number of issues.

At Washington and Cornell universities, several colleagues have taken an interest in my work. I would like to thank Martin Bloom, William Butterfield, Shanti Khinduka, John Morris, Martha Ozawa, Aaron Rosen, William Short, Herbert Staulcup, and Paul Stuart. I am especially grateful to Richard Campbell and Stanley Witkin. I would like to express my gratitude to the folks in the Social Analyses of Science Systems (SASS) program at Cornell for providing the resources that made the writing of this possible. Robert McGinnis and Alice Terlouw have been particularly helpful. David Margolis has been very helpful with editorial assistance. I would also like to thank Floyd Bolitho,

Robert Porter, and LeRoy Schultz for their help in the beginning.

This book was conceived in collaboration with my twin brother Buck, who has since taken up other interests. However, a major part of the early data collection and analysis was done with his help. Brian Cochran has also been most helpful to this research. I would like to close with a special thanks to my second self, Buck, for his contribution to the direction this report has taken. Of course, none of these innocent colleagues and friends is responsible for errors, distortions, or omissions. In fact, a number of them have expressed disagreement with at least part of the analysis that follows. I am indebted to them for sharing their views with me.

I would like to thank the American Psychological Association for permission to use material from previous papers published in the *American Psychologist* and the editor of *Quality and Quantity* for permission to use material published in that journal.

Eugene, Oregon   DUNCAN LINDSEY
August 1978

Contents

Tables and Figures

Tables

Figures

The Author

DUNCAN LINDSEY is a postdoctoral fellow in the Social Systems Research Program, Department of Sociology, at Cornell University and an assistant professor at the School of Community Service and Public Affairs, University of Oregon at Eugene. His undergraduate studies were completed at the University of California, Santa Cruz, where he received a bachelor's degree (1969) in psychology and sociology. He earned his master's degree (1971) in social science education at Antioch College and his interdisciplinary doctor's degree (1973) in sociology, psychiatry, and social work at Northwestern University.

Lindsey is the author of *Children of the Asylum* (1977). He is founder and editor of *Children and Youth Services Review* and a cofounder of the *Journal of Social Service Research*. He has published numerous articles in the fields of psychology, social work, and sociology and is an elected member of the editorial and publications committee of the Society for the Study of Social Problems. Defining himself as a social worker with broad interdisciplinary interests, Lindsey focuses his principal research and teaching activities on psychopharmacology, social policies regarding mental health, and social work education.

Lindsey lives in Eugene, Oregon, with his wife, Deborah, and their son, Ethan. His favorite leisure activity is backpacking into the wilderness.

To Deborah McDaniel-Lindsey
whose love and teachings have made
this book and so much more possible.

The Scientific Publication System in Social Science

*A Study of the Operation
of Leading Professional Journals
in Psychology, Sociology, and Social Work*

1

Publication in Social Science

Science is a very human form of knowledge. We are always at the brink of the known, we always feel forward for what is to be hoped. Every judgment in science stands on the edge of error and is personal. Science is a tribute to what we can know although we are fallible. In the end the words were said by Oliver Cromwell: "I beseech you, in the bowels of Christ, think it possible you may be mistaken."

—Bronowski, 1973, p. 374

The spirit and contribution of science is captured and conveyed through the scientific publication system. The present work is concerned with that publication system for both practical and theoretical purposes. On the practical side, my interest is to present useful information to the practicing scientist who regularly confronts the scientific communication system in the course of his or her own work. My theoretical interest is to examine critically the adequacy of current sociological models of science, models in which the scientific publication system is a vital subunit.

On the Practical Side

The journal publication system is one of the most crucial institutions in science. The decisions made by the editorial boards

1

of these journals are fundamental to the professional lives of scientists, for the performance of a scientist is judged mainly in terms of publication. Further, the scientist's ability to share his or her findings and to establish priority are both controlled through the journal publication system. In essence, the products of a scientist's labor are assessed and distributed through the scientific publication system.

In professional and graduate school, scientists are trained in the most advanced methods of research, analysis, and scholarship. This is as it should be. However, little attention is given to how the results of this high-quality work are distributed to the larger scientific community. As a result, scientists are frequently naive about the gatekeeper functions of the scientific publication system; what knowledge they have is usually of the *folk* variety.

In this book, my concern is to unveil the scientific publication system, to open it up for critical scrutiny so that members of the professions may both use it more effectively and work knowledgeably to improve it. The mystique that surrounds the scientific publication system is, by and large, unwarranted. It has developed partly because of the closed and confidential operation of editorial review boards. Nonetheless, it is a rational system that serves the needs of the modern scientific enterprise in disseminating information.

On the Theoretical Side

What underlies and is a common thread throughout my efforts is a set of values regarding the proper conduct of activities in science. I take seriously the idea that science, and here I refer to the social and behavioral sciences especially, ought to be universalistic, open, and guided by compassionate and concerned scholarship. In fulfilling this ideal, science is responsive to both the wider community it serves and to the members of the scientific community. The introduction of particularistic biases (such as friendship, nepotism, and affiliation) reduces the contribution of science, antagonizes segments of the community, and creates a moral climate of despair.

In his pioneering theoretical work in the sociology of science, Merton (1973) has argued quite forcefully that the social system governing the behavior and mobility of scientists is characterized by an extraordinarily high degree of objectivity and fairness. I am dissatisfied with this *normative* model of science, for the norms identified by Merton do not appear to be applied uniformly in any kind of science I am familiar with. It is especially in the social and behavioral sciences that his idealistic picture seems to me excessively respectful. My preference, in this regard, is for the iconoclasm of Ravetz (1971) or Kuhn (1962).

Jonathan and Stephan Cole (1973) have done a good deal of empirical work to examine the normative theoretical model outlined by their mentor Merton. By and large, their findings have confirmed his. However, their research has been limited by some rather important methodological shortcomings. For example, they use a cross-sectional design when a longitudinal study would have been more appropriate. In addition, their findings are to a large extent an artifact of their instruments, especially in their reliance on citation counts as a measure of quality in science. Although the Coles have suggested that their findings, which are derived primarily from the study of physics, are with slight modification applicable to the social and behavioral sciences, the findings of others, such as Blume (1974), Law (1974), Mahoney (1977), and Yoels (1971, 1974), as well as the present work, raise fundamental doubts regarding the adequacy of the normative model of science, especially in its application to the social and behavioral sciences. The work of an increasing number of investigators suggests that nonscientific criteria play a much greater role than has previously been recognized. Nowhere is this intrusion of nonscientific criteria more evident than in the subsystem of science responsible for publication.

Why does Merton's idealistic model for the social structure and prevailing ethos in the hard sciences fail to accurately portray the character of the scientific enterprise in the social and behavioral sciences? There are several reasons. First, there is a lack of paradigm development and consensus in the social and behavioral sciences (see Lodahl and Gordon, 1972; Hagstrom, 1970; Freese, 1972; Pfeffer, Leong, and Strehl, 1977).

Second, the social and behavioral sciences deal with *social reality*, which has deep roots in political, economic, and class concerns (Gouldner, 1970). While the physical and biological sciences may sometimes be open to political and cultural controversies, physical and biological reality is invariant across national and political boundaries. However, social order, social structure, and thus social reality are quite different across these boundaries. Social reality is not the same in China, Sweden, Poland, and the United States. The social and behavioral sciences, because they are based on political and cultural assumptions, are unable to invent the value-free, objective criteria that obtain in the physical sciences. Of necessity, social science activity in various countries reflects prevailing ideologies (compare, for example, the great differences in rates of citations to the work of Karl Marx by social and behavioral scientists in communist countries and in democracies—see Applebaum, 1978).

Third, as a result of the spectacular industrial and technological successes of the physical and biological sciences, the wider community has supported the institutions of science (Kevles, 1971). The social and behavioral sciences have benefited indirectly from these efforts (following, as it were, on the coattails of these accomplishments). However, there have been less spectacular translations of social and behavioral science knowledge into serviceable programs or products (Scribner and Chalk, 1977; MacRae, 1976). The results of social and behavioral science activity reflect the political and ideological views of the working scientists, and the implementation of new programs often requires some transformation of social reality. Resistance and the lack of acceptance of some social and behavioral science knowledge by the general community, as well as controversy within the social and behavioral science community, are other factors that alter social structure and professional behavior in the social sciences.

I should emphasize here my belief that the social and behavioral sciences are sufficiently different from the physical sciences to require a separate analytic model. Unless otherwise stated, from now on when I speak of science I will be talking only about the social and behavioral sciences, without intending to generalize the discussion to the physical and biological sciences.

An Outline of Things to Come

The next chapter examines the history of scientific journals and the functions they have come to provide in various fields. It contains an examination of the responsibility journals carry for both (1) the fostering of scientific inquiry, dialogue, and debate and (2) the professional regulation and control of controversy.

The decision-making organization of journal editors and referees serves both as a filtration system for the dissemination of ideas among professionals and as a mechanism for overseeing scientific research. Chapter Three presents data from a cross-disciplinary survey of the criteria used in assessing the quality of scientific papers. The interpretation and application of these criteria by journal editors governs the approaches to methodology and scholarly inquiry in the sciences. Since the decisions of the journal editors have such important consequences for the careers of scientists, the findings in this chapter are germane to the broader studies of social stratification in science.

The survey of journal editors reported in Chapter Three indicates that the most important criterion for publication is the *value of an author's finding to the field*. Chapter Four addresses the question, "How is value determined?" It is *not* a technical assessment that can be made by a well-trained clerk. Rather, it requires the judgment of an expert in the field. In fact, since there is often disagreement even among distinguished scientists, the decision is usually made by several reviewers and then conveyed to the author as a corporate response of the editorial board. In large measure, the quality of a journal is reflected in the caliber of its review board. Who are the editorial board members who sit in judgment on the quality or publishability of submitted research? What qualifies editorial board members to make these decisions? Data from an archival study of the scientific accomplishments of editorial board members in various fields, as measured by number of publications produced and citations attracted, indicate a variation in staffing patterns across the fields, with important implications for the quality and standards of editorial review boards.

Chapter Three discusses the ideal criteria used by editorial boards. Chapter Five examines the criteria that actually operate in publication review proceedings. Although there is a high degree of consensus regarding the ideal criteria, substantial disagreement occurs in the application of these criteria. This divergence is often explained as the result of the intrusion of nonscientific standards (the personality of the author, prestige characteristics, and so on) and the methodological and ideological biases of the reviewer. I present a review and assessment of the conflicting studies in this controversial area and introduce data from my own research that have rather important implications for policies governing the operation of professional journals.

Chapter Six examines a random sample of 1,179 articles from several social and bioscience fields in a detailed empirical study. I have collected a great deal of information on these articles, such as the estimated number of words, the number of references, the use of quantitative methods, acknowledgment of funding, and number of tables and graphs. In addition, I have followed these articles, all of which were published in 1970, in the citation indexes from 1970 to 1976 in order to discern whether they have structural characteristics that can predict their impact or use.

Chapter Seven takes a careful look at the shortcomings of the scientific publication system and discusses their possible consequences for the vitality and achievement of science. I also explore such strategies for solving or minimizing these problems as multiple submission, reduced publication review time, page fees, submission fees, multiple reviews, and author appeal procedures.

The closing remarks briefly summarize the themes of the book and tie the important elements of the separate chapters into an integrated view of the scientific publication system, with particular attention to those factors the scientist should understand when he or she engages the system.

The Measurement Note at the end of the book contains a discussion of the assessment of quality by citations, one of the more important, but narrowly focused, technical problems plaguing empirical studies in the sociology of science. This issue arises several times during the course of the present book; I have treated it at length at the end, rather than in the main body of the text, so as not to distract that part of my audience not professionally concerned with it.

2

Professional Journals in Science

━━━━━━━━━━━

Journals were intermediaries through which a succession of remarks, attacks, and replies could be published and noised throughout the learned world. . . . By their criticisms and threats of exposing plagiaries, inaccuracies, and other defects, by removing scholars from the condition of privacy and isolation, and by the vast panorama of objective learning which journals spread before savants, learned periodicals contributed to the sum total of the critical element in the intellectual life of Europe.

—Barnes, 1934, p. 259

At the beginnings of secular inquiry into the nature of the physical world, scholars and scientists relied on letters of correspondence to communicate their results to each other (Kronick, 1976). In this early period of science, mail systems were slow and irregular. The letters of correspondence, frequently difficult to read and even more difficult to obtain, restricted access to available scientific knowledge to a relatively few participants.

In the middle of the seventeenth century, typeset periodicals began to emerge as the primary means of disseminating scientific information. The early periodicals were quite general in scope and appealed to an upper-class literary public as well as to scientists. Further, the early scientists were amateurs. Universities and government research laboratories had not yet developed to sponsor research as an occupation (Ben-David, 1972).

The most important participants in the earlier letters of correspondence served as editors of the new journals. The early periodicals were characterized by short publication lives, with few lasting more than five years. The average time between the acceptance of a paper and its subsequent publication was about three years (Kronick, 1976, p. 162). Before the new journals established routine review procedures, there were numerous abuses surrounding the review process. The notorious case of the famous mathematician Cauchy is illustrative. Ravetz (1971, p. 256) writes, "On receiving a paper for refereeing, he [Cauchy] could not resist the temptation of recasting the proof, improving the result, developing and generalizing it in all sorts of ways, and finally publishing it in a journal to which he had rapid access."

At first the journals published papers on a wide variety of topics. With the growing differentiation of scientific disciplines, however, specialized societies emerged. These early scientific societies were the centers of scientific dialogue and interchange. Since the published literature in this period was small, the major forum for the presentation of ideas or research findings was at the meetings of the societies. In publishing their proceedings, the early societies gave rise to more narrowly focused scientific journals. Since the published papers had been subject to critical scrutiny during presentation at meetings of the society, their subsequent publication gave them an authority not previously associated with journal publication (Ornstein, 1938). Thus the journals were held responsible for their contents, and a primary task of the early editors was to screen out inadequate contributions.

The major growth of scientific periodicals occurred during the last half of the eighteenth century. Kronick (1976, p. 78) reports that the number of scientific periodicals rose from 52 in 1749 to 416 in 1789. This sudden rise can be traced, not to improvements in either technology or postal systems, but to an expansion of scientific research facilitated by the emergence of universities and the growth of science as a profession. With the expansion of scientific research, the channels for communicating the products of that research also expanded.

The Function of Professional Journals

The history of scientific journals provides a background for understanding their current structure and operation, for the five major functions of the modern scientific journal may be found in embryonic form in the earliest periodicals. These are (1) collection of the products of scientific and scholarly inquiry, (2) selection of those to be published, (3) publication of selected materials, (4) distribution of published materials, and (5) storage of the published work for posterity.

These tasks have been allocated to separate groups in the scientific communication system. Editorial boards, filling the role of the early correspondents, are responsible for collecting and selecting manuscripts for publication. Publishers are responsible for the printing and distribution of the manuscripts selected by the editorial boards. Whereas the primary motive of the editorial board is the advancement of knowledge and the control of ideas, the motive of the publisher is to make a profit. The university presses and scientific societies, with their non-profit status, are only partial exceptions to this (Lane, 1970).

The storage function of the journal is the responsibility of archival, library, and, more recently, information specialists. Publication, distribution, and storage are beyond the scope and interest of this inquiry. In the chapters that follow, I will be concentrating on the editorial review boards—their composition, attitudes, and performance. The decisions of the editorial review boards affect scientists directly.

The Function of Editorial Review Boards

Editorial review boards have always been responsible, through the screening out of inadequate or improper contributions, for defending the scientific literature from charlatans. An article published in a scientific journal carries with it the approval of the board of editors, who certify its validity. As Gustin (1973, p. 1126) has remarked, "Publication, including the referee system, is science's instrument of assessment and validation and confirms a contribution as scientific; that is, as true, thus linking the individual to the community and its tradition." Consequently, publication is evidence of the performance of legitimate scientific study. However, with increasing demands on limited publication space, especially in the social sciences, editorial boards, in addition to maintaining legitimacy, became responsible for determining standards of excellence required for publication.

There is also a prestige hierarchy among the journals in each field. Hawkins, Ritter, and Walter (1973, p. 1017) write, "The question that invariably follows the author's cheery statement 'Guess what. . . . my paper was accepted!' is 'Where?' And the expressions of the assembled faces unfailingly mirror the answer." The scientist who is able to have his or her work published in a prestigious journal, where many colleagues may see it, will thereby increase his or her eligibility for promotion, tenure, or other professional rewards (Tuckman, 1976).

There have been numerous studies of the prestige of journals within different fields, such as sociology (Glenn, 1971; Roche and Smith, 1976), psychology (Buss and McDermott, 1976; Koulack and Kesselman, 1975; Mace and Warner, 1973), economics (Moore, 1972; Hawkins, Ritter, and Walter, 1973), political science (Giles and Wright, 1975), and physics (Inhaber, 1974). The Institute for Scientific Information issues an annual ranking of the journals covered in the *Science Citation Index* based on their number of citations (Garfield, 1972).

The prestige hierarchy among scientific journals has led to the selective dissemination of information with the better papers going to the more prestigious journals (Stinchcombe, 1976). This selectivity permits easy location of important material, but it also creates the possibility that important material of a highly specialized nature could be lost, tucked away in an obscure specialized journal. Further, the power to distribute information is greatly concentrated in a few central publications.

The prestige rankings of the journals in the different fields need to be viewed with a certain amount of healthy skepticism.

own work. Over the years, even before the work of Mitroff, Merton (1977) began to modify his quite optimistic portrait of the behavior of scientists. Mahoney's experimental studies (1977, 1978) raise questions regarding adherence to the idealistic norms outlined by Merton. Yet Zuckerman (1977) suggests that among the *best* scientists (in her study, American Nobel laureates) there is a zealous pursuit of these norms. Zuckerman (1977, pp. 126-127), writes, "The elite apprentices of elite scientists internalized exacting standards of work through several related social processes. They emulated the masters whose own work exemplified those standards, they were led to see things they did not know they knew and to have ideas of a kind they had not had before through the evocative behavior of the master, and they experienced these elevated standards in practice by having their own work severely evaluated."

In contrast to other forms of scientific communication, such as books, the scientific journal allows critical discussion and dialogue. In many of the journals, comments, letters to the editor, and dialogues with authors are the most exciting and energetic sections, revealing the passionate side of science. At the same time, they reveal the extent of disagreement among the members of the scientific community. They demonstrate that even papers that have passed through the highly selective review process are not beyond criticism. (Fortunately for the authors of these papers, their critics were not the readers before publication—or perhaps unfortunately.)

Nowhere is the lack of consensus among scientists more evident than in the book review journals. Book publishers usually have a manuscript read by several commissioned referees. The book is placed under close critical scrutiny. Since they publish fewer than one in every hundred submitted manuscripts, scholarly and scientific book publishers can afford to be very selective (Powell, in press).

Nonetheless, many of the published books are reviewed unfavorably. Clearly, many books would not have been published had negative scholarly evaluations been available to the publishers. I mention this to alert the reader to the wide divergence in assessment of scientific work even among eminent scientists.

3

Criteria for the Evaluation of Manuscripts

━━━━━━━━━━━━━━━━

The responses indicated that most journals do have vaguely documented standards for acceptance and rejection of papers. These standards, however, seem confined to the minds of the editors, are poorly documented, and are not communicated to readers or prospective authors.
—Benedik, 1976, p. 90

Professional journal editors and their referees are the gatekeepers of the public forum of a profession. They control access to the public dissemination and discussion of ideas. As a result of this power, they also act as gatekeepers for the higher echelons of the academic profession (see Crane, 1967; Cole and Cole, 1973), and their decisions are critical to the careers of aspiring young scholars and researchers. What criteria do professional journal editorial board members use when examining a manuscript submitted for publication? Several studies have suggested that there are technical norms of the scientific craft in each discipline and that a manuscript is judged against these norms (Whitley, 1970a; Smigel and Ross, 1970). This chapter examines these norms and their interpretation by journal editors and referees in psychology, social work, and sociology.

15

Criteria for Editorial Decision Making

How effectively does the decision-making structure of journal editorial boards serve to disseminate ideas and advance learning? The answer to this question has important consequences for the growth and prosperity of the scientific community, for the quality and productivity of research is determined in large part by the effective functioning of the stratification system of science, which is in turn predominantly controlled by the editorial boards.

To study the screening function of editorial boards, investigators have concentrated on the factors influencing the decision-making process. However, the major thrust of these investigations has been directed toward factors other than the normative criteria. An example of this approach is Whitley's (1970a) study of the operations of two British social science journals. His investigation focused on four factors relating to editorial decisions: (1) the professional attributes of authors submitting manuscripts, (2) the kinds of papers they submit, (3) the professional qualifications of the editorial referees who advise the editors, and (4) the amount of time for editorial judgments. Whitley's findings suggest that these factors have little, if any, measurable influence on the decisions of editors. Smigel and Ross (1970) report similar findings in their case study of editorial decision making by a sociology journal. Overall, the few sociological studies available provide limited support for any suspicion that factors other than the normative criteria substantially influence editorial judgments (McCartney, 1978). Crane (1967) finds a small, but statistically significant, measurable influence of nonscientific factors—either personal bias or mutual socialization—on editoral decision making. In their study of publication in the physics community, Cole and Cole (1973) demonstrate that universalistic standards of evaluation dominate almost to the exclusion of particularistic standards; however, Yoels (1974) reports a greatly reduced prevalence of universalistic standards for social science publication. Pfeffer, Leong, and Strehl (1977) bridge these results by taking into account the variations in paradigm development within fields.

Trustees of the Normative Criteria

To evaluate a manuscript submitted for publication, editors and referees employ the normative criteria of scientific inquiry. Chase (1970) examined the interpretations of the normative criteria made by professors in sixteen selected departments at a "Big Ten" university. To identify the norms, Chase developed a list of criteria drawn from several sources and asked the professors to rate them. Her findings from a sample of 191 professors reveal extensive agreement on the importance of all criteria. However, she did find significant differences in the ratings of individual items between professors in the natural and social sciences: "Natural scientists placed more emphasis on the qualities of replicability of research techniques, originality, mathematical precision, and coverage of the literature, whereas social scientists gave higher ranking to logical rigor, theoretical significance, and applied significance" (Chase, 1970, p. 263).

The Chase research illuminates what criteria govern scientific inquiry and reveals that the normative criteria are not a codified body of technical standards but a fluid system of values that range between empirical inquiry and creative theory development. Wolff (1970) suggests that there are also differences in emphasis on the normative criteria among the social science disciplines.

What are the particular emphases of the institutionalized interpreters of normative criteria—the journal editors and their referees? Whitley (1970b, p. 246) reports, "Perceptions of quality by editorial referees are influenced by the dominant technical norms of the area." But, beyond technical matters, the journal editors and their referees are trusted to apply the artistic and research values of the scientific craft. The journal editors do not legislate the normative criteria of the field: The normative criteria emerge through an ongoing process of symbolic interaction and negotiation among the dominant culture, the subcultures of the field, and the journal editors, who are members of the scientific subcultures (Law, 1974; Crane, 1972). Their interpretations of these norms, however, govern the growth and development of various approaches to the scientific craft.

Research Values: Elements of the Normative Criteria

According to Cole and Cole (1973, p. 77), there is "a relatively high level of consensus as to what constitutes outstanding work, what are important problems to be addressed, and what are acceptable empirical techniques for testing scientific theories." Available research studies indicate the normative criteria are the most important influence on editorial decision making (Wolff, 1970; Gustin, 1973). However, since the criteria were given different emphases by professors, we may expect this same difference in emphasis among journal editors, even though a basic core of values exists.

I propose that the normative criteria are more accurately viewed as research values. The major difference in research orientation in the social and behavioral sciences is between the qualitative and quantitative methodologist, sometimes termed the *soft* and *hard* methodologists. How real and strong is this difference? Is there also a difference in research values among the various social and behavioral sciences? For instance, do the editors of sociology journals express a different normative emphasis from that expressed by psychology or social work editors? If so, such a difference should provide clues to the substantive variations between the disciplines themselves.

An Investigation of Editors' Research Values

I have suggested that journal editors may have a spectrum of values concerning the scientific craft. To examine this spectrum, I conducted a self-report survey of journal editorial board members to determine their emphases when reviewing a submitted manuscript. Borrowing from the previous work of Chase (1970), Smigel and Ross (1970), and Wolff (1970, 1973), I developed a checklist inventory of research values, containing twelve items considered fundamental criteria of scientific inquiry (see Table 1). Editors were asked to rate these values on a continuum from "of highest importance" (with a score of 7) to "less important" (score of 1).

TABLE 1. Journal Editors' Ranking of Normative Criteria for Scientific Craftsmanship.

Criterion	Mean	Standard Deviation
The value of the author's findings to the advancement of the field	5.82	1.35
The grasp of the author's research design on the question investigated	5.56	1.36
The theoretical relevance of the question investigated	5.42	1.44
The scholarship demonstrated in the article	5.39	1.52
The creativity of ideas in the article	5.18	1.47
The presence of original empirical evidence	4.96	1.59
The sophistication of the author's research methodology and data analysis	4.34	1.69
The relevance of the article to the journal's focus	4.25	1.69
The ethical sense demonstrated by the author	4.14	2.06
The value of the article's findings to the affairs of everyday social life	2.89	1.88
The entertainment quality of the essay	1.51	1.07
The background and reputation of the author [a]	1.33	0.86

NOTE: N = 265.

[a] The policy of anonymous review employed by the majority of journals may be responsible for much of this last rating.

The sample frame for the study consisted of editorial board members of professional journals in the fields of psychology, social work, and sociology. Approximately 100 editors of journals in each field were selected, for a total sample of 323. The journals selected were representative of their respective disciplines.

There are few national journals of social work. The cluster sample included every known national social work journal, including four that previous researchers had identified as representative of the field (Weinberger and Tripodi, 1969). Those selected were *Child Welfare, Clinical Social Work Journal, Journal of Education for Social Work, Social Casework, Social Service Review, Social Work,* and *Urban and Social Change Review.* To ensure equal representation among disciplines, the size of the social work subsample determined the size of the others. (Several members of the *Child Welfare* editorial board did not have the editorial decision-making power assumed in this chapter. The editorial boards of *Social Service Review* and *Social Forces* were composed of two subgroups, similar to the board structure of the *American Journal of Sociology.* The editor members in the first major subgrouping were included in the sample.)

Six sociology journals were randomly selected from the first 25 American sociology journals in Glenn's (1971) listing of the 63 major journals of the profession: *American Sociological Review, American Sociologist, The Journal of Health and Social Behavior, Sociology of Education, Social Forces,* and *Social Problems.*

From the American Psychological Association's listing of sponsored journals, five psychology journals were randomly selected: *Journal of Abnormal Psychology, Journal of Applied Psychology, Journal of Counseling Psychology, Journal of Educational Psychology,* and *Journal of Personality and Social Psychology.*

All editorial board members of the selected journals were sent a checklist questionnaire. Several of the psychology journals had unusually large editorial boards; a random drawing of twenty board members was made for these journals.

Data from this cluster sample were collected by self-administered mail questionnaire. The strength of this method of data collection has been demonstrated by Dillman and his colleagues (1974); several of their innovative follow-up techniques were employed in this survey. The initial checklist was mailed with a self-addressed return envelope. Four weeks after the initial mailing, a follow-up letter with a replacement questionnaire was sent to nonrespondents. If there was no response in seven weeks, a second letter with a replacement questionnaire was sent by certified mail. This strategy achieved an excellent return rate, averaging 82 percent, which accounts for N = 265 in Table 1.

The editors' range of preference among the items, seen in the standard deviations in Table 1, indicates that there is a limited consensus on principal standards. To isolate item preference patterns in order to define principal components that account for the maximum number of individual differences, a factor analysis was applied (Overall and Klett, 1972). Three factors were extracted using a principal components analysis with oblique rotations, as Mulaik (1972) advocates, in order to examine the relationship between principal components extracted by the factor analysis.

Table 2 displays the oblique rotation's factor pattern and structure matrices. The first two factors derived by the oblique solution represent the quantitative and qualitative methodological orientations hypothesized. The pattern matrix shows that the two items that have substantial loadings on the first or quantitative factor are *grasp of design* and *sophistication of methodology*. There is a modest loading on *scholarship,* while the presence of *empirical evidence* recorded a smaller but moderate loading. Taken together, these four items represent the underlying dimensions of quantitative methodological orientation.

The factor structure provides the correlation coefficients of the individual items with the derived factors displayed in the factor pattern matrix. There is a close correspondence between the factor loadings and the correlation coefficients for the quantitative factor. The largest difference is with theoretical relevance. Although this item does not record a moderate loading in the factor pattern, it does have a moderate positive correlation with the factor. This suggests that the quantitative orientation is not divorced from a concern with theoretical relevance.

The second factor characterizes the qualitative methodological orientation. The items that have substantial loadings on it are theoretical relevance and creativity of ideas. The item scholarship registers a moderate loading. Although it records only a slightly moderate loading, the item value of the author's findings to the field has its largest loading on this factor.

TABLE 2. Research Values of Journal Editorial Board Members.

Research Value [a]	Factor Pattern			Factor Structure		
	Factor 1	Factor 2	Factor 3	Factor 1	Factor 2	Factor 3
Theory relevance	.13788	.57782	-.03348	.33347	.62093	.08941
Empirical evidence	.30837	.10290	.00348	.34530	.21180	.08846
Scholarship	.48057	.30045	-.15129	.55251	.44516	.00350
Creativity of ideas	-.14329	.57127	.09231	.07796	.53565	.15164
Value of findings	.06110	.25978	.01719	.15621	.28400	.07225
Ethical sense	.16191	.04665	.31496	.24832	.15382	.35840
Grasp of design	.69410	-.14265	.18780	.68572	.13121	.31934
Value to social life	-.06538	.07173	.92135	.16465	.19583	.91827
Sophistication of methods	.58811	-.02389	.00962	.58185	.18429	.13655

iterations = 25

NOTE: Oblique rotations with Kaiser normalization and delta = 0.0 (Harman, 1967).

[a] Items that are not elements of the normative criteria of scientific craftsmanship or that had a grossly skewed distribution were not included after analysis showed them to be irrelevant.

The third factor derived from the oblique rotation loaded extremely heavily on the item value of the author's findings to social life and moderately on ethical sense. The underlying dimension measured by this factor is thus limited primarily to one item. The factor analysis suggests that this is a separate dimension of the factor space, which is not part of the other two factors. However, the limited scope of this factor restricts its utility as a composite index.

The first two factors are representative of the quantitative and qualitative methodological orientations hypothesized. The differences in research orientations revealed through the factor analysis revolve around the styles of the scientific craft emphasized by editorial reviewers. The factor analysis shows that several of the items locate together into distinctive cluster-centroid structures within the factor space (Overall and Klett, 1972). The varying degrees of importance placed on these derived factors reflects the research style emphasized by the editorial referee.

The questionnaire also included an item that asked the editorial board member if he or she placed a greater emphasis on qualitative rather than on quantitative methodology. The responses of the editors to this question confirm that the journal board members do place a greater emphasis on quantitative rather than on qualitative methodology (89 preferring the latter, 108 preferring the former). However, the dispersion in emphasis among the editors is fairly normal.

What is the relationship between the quantitative and qualitative factor dimensions? The primary advantage of the oblique factor solution is that it permits an exploration of the relationship between the derived factors. The correlation between the quantitative and qualitative factor dimensions is substantial ($r = .35$), which indicates these are not disparate dimensions. Further, it would seem that the question about a qualitative or quantitative emphasis assumed these to be opposite ends of a polarized single dimension that did not emerge in the factor analysis. Several respondents had a difficult time with the emphasis preference question. In fact, several of the editors' additional comments focused on the difficulties the presumed polarity raised. The following comments are illustrative:

Qualitative research methods are, in my opinion, preferable for some purposes while quantitative methods are preferable for others. If I receive a paper reporting a study with quantitative methods, I try to judge it according to the standards appropriate for such studies, even though I have used qualitative methods in most of my own research.

* * *

What I value is the author's ability to *suit* data collection and processing to the nature of the questions he raises and tries to answer and vice versa. That is, I judge the author's ability to fit questions to available data and its manipulation.

The qualitative and quantitative dimensions both share a concern for scholarship. Both factor dimensions represent particular styles of the scientific craft that are not mutually exclusive. In fact, this analysis would indicate that they could be, and frequently are, complementary—not opposite ends of a continuum but positively correlated, separate dimensions of the normative criteria of the scientific craft. Qualitative methodology is not inherently more efficient than quantitative methodology. Quantitative methods are not inherently better than qualitative methods. Both have their places in the research arsenal of the skilled scientific investigator.

Methodological Orientation and Contribution to the Field

Before we leave this discussion of the patterns located by the oblique factor rotations, one last point needs to be examined. The most important criterion for publication, in terms of overall mean item scores, was the *value of an author's findings to the field.* Few journals outline criteria for publication. However, the American Psychological Association's *Publication Manual* (1974, p. 101) provides the following information under the section "Selection of manuscripts": "A manuscript is judged by three main criteria: (1) it must make a significant contribution to an area of psychology appropriate to the journal to which it is submitted; (2) it must convey its message clearly and as briefly as its content permits; and (3) it must be in a form that will maintain the journal's integrity of style. Manuscripts that do not meet the first requirement are rejected. Those that do not fully meet the second requirement but are otherwise considered acceptable are returned to the author for revision. Those that do not meet the third requirement may be returned for revision prior to editorial consideration."

If the criterion of a significant contribution to the field is not met, the article is rejected. This finding corresponds to the findings in Scott's study (1974, p. 701) of the editorial review process at the *Journal of Personality and Social Psychology:* "From these data, soundness of design and judged 'importance' of the contribution seem to be considerations that most commonly affect manuscript appraisal." Determination of contribution to the field calls for the greatest skill in judgment and thus requires the assessment of a distinguished scientist. Most of the other criteria are, in large measure, technical norms and could be evaluated by a well-trained clerk using a standardized evaluation checklist (Wolff, 1973). But the criterion of value of the author's finding to the field requires the reviewer's judgment of the investigator's contribution to the normative paradigms of the field or of the introduction of a crucial critique of the normative paradigms (Law, 1974). Only those intimately involved in the paradigms of the field, who have achieved distinction working with these paradigms, are adequate judges for this kind of work. This is why journal editorial board members are generally distinguished contributors to their field. The positive judgment of these referees confers the prestige associated with publication in their respective journals.

This crucial criterion of the value of the author's findings did record a loading, albeit small, in the qualitative dimension and almost no loading in the quantitative dimension. This would suggest that qualitative methodological emphasis reflects a greater concern with the value of the findings to the field.

Surely it would be fair to suggest that quantitative researchers are more tightly constrained by their methodology than qualitative researchers. It is here, within the intellectual skyscrapers of his or her mathematical achievements, that the social science architect has the highest probability of losing sight of the explanatory mission of the analysis. It is a difficult and rewarding process to keep quantitative methodology on the track of assessing social science explanations. Quantitative methodology requires the transformation of fluid social reality into relatively static quantum reality that can be mapped out and explained in terms of probability statements. The requirements of data characteristics and quality, along with their attendant assumptions for subsequent manipulations, are still quite rigorous. Frequently, in translating social reality into quantum reality in order to develop mathematical models of explanation, many of the specifically "human," nonquantitative elements of life are washed out. However, what is lost, is, one hopes, gained in terms of greater precision (see Costner and Leik, 1964).

The Additional Comments of Editorial Board Members

All of the items on the research value checklist are important to an evaluation of a manuscript. Several of the editorial board members commented on the questionnaire that most of these elements are critical—that their absence or clear deficiency might immediately preclude a favorable recommendation for publication. In addition, several board members suggested criteria they employ in their assessments other than those on the checklist questionnaire. In their own words, these include:

> I also value highly a systematic comprehension of a molar phenomenon and an expressed awareness of how the necessarily limited data collected fit into the broader aspects of the general problem.
>
> *   *   *
>
> There is also something that might be called "intellectual naiveté" that shows through in the author's style—usually in the first paragraph. On the other hand, its complement—intellectual sophistication—is not always so quickly identified in a paragraph or two."
>
> *   *   *

Generalizability of results is important. This is somewhat subjective, of course, but any study is trivial if [it] has no rationale for extrapolating findings to other conditions, situations, environments with some sense of boundary range of generalizability at some subjective confidence level. This is related to—but not equivalent to—theory relevance.

* * *

I have refereed enough papers for the *American Sociological Review* and *Sociometry* to know that not a few authors deliberately distort their presentation so as to make a failure appear as a success. It is my personal value judgment that there is nothing more despicable and offensive to the scientific enterprise, which, at rock bottom, is concerned with discovering the truth.

* * *

The big fat fallacy is an elaborate methodology that bears not at all on the real question. The trouble is so often that the authors have read nothing, literally nothing, written before 1960. They therefore rediscover the wheel. I am obviously an old fart in your factor space. I do gruff on a third issue, though: good ideas well written, not thesis committee genuflection to method. Yet I also think every journal should be *archival*, dedicated to knowledge, not "how to" manuals.

On a more critical note, one reviewer commented, "My objection to this kind of research is very deep and would require a greater expenditure of time than I can now afford to indicate it to you. Suffice to say that it proceeds on a base of assumptions which are untested and/or inapplicable. Just let me mention a few: (a) It assumes an ordered set of competitive criteria applied to each paper being judged. I know of no such definitive criteria in my case. I would have to construct them in order to answer your questions, an ex post facto act. (b) Your scale appears to assume unidistant grades, but I have no way of making my judgments of importance on the spatial metaphor."

Approaches to Knowledge Building Across the Disciplines

The journal editorial board members reported diverse emphases in their interpretations of the normative criteria of the scientific craft. Chase (1970) differentiated these emphases for natural and social scientists. I have hypothesized that similar differences would be found among social scientists and between social science disciplines. The data reveal that a divergence in emphasis emerges in the factor analysis and in the response to the question of methodological preference. In order to examine this variation across disciplines, the editors' responses to the methodological preference question were cross tabulated within the separate disciplines. The results are displayed in Table 3.

TABLE 3.   Methodological Preferences of Journal
Editors Across Disciplines.

Place a Greater Emphasis on Qualitative Methodology—Response	Field of Journal		
	Sociology	Social Work	Psychology
Strongly agree	4 (5.0%)	23 (30.0%)	9 (11.5%)
Agree	9 (11.3%)	25 (32.5%)	19 (24.4%)
Unsure	16 (20.0%)	8 (10.4%)	14 (17.9%)
Disagree	37 (46.3%)	15 (19.5%)	19 (24.4%)
Strongly disagree	14 (17.5%)	6 (7.8%)	17 (21.8%)
	80	77	78

NOTE: Likelihood ratio χ^2 43.09; $p < .001$ with 8 df; $N = 235$.

The data indicate a significant difference in methodological preference across disciplines. The major difference is the stronger qualitative emphasis among social work editorial board members. The opposite is the case in both sociology and psychology journals.

Social Work.   The differences in methodological preferences among the disciplines may derive from the nature of their subject matter. Specifically, the differences observed here may be the result of the status of research in the social work profession (Germain, 1971). Aaron Rosenblatt (1968), examining the utilization of research by social workers in agencies, discovered that research findings were eschewed by practitioners. When confronted with a difficult case, social workers look last to research for assistance. Also, social workers rank course work in research as the least useful preparation for their actual job performance (Rosenblatt, 1968). Since qualitative methodology is a more palatable form of research for nonresearchers, social work editors may place a greater emphasis on it to suit their readers.

There is evidence to suggest that understanding of simple statistics is marginal, if not critically inadequate, even among social work researchers (Weed and Greenwald, 1973). This suggests either inadequate preparation in research or an unsympathetic posture toward quantitative methodology. Several observers have lamented these influences on the current status of research in social work (Kahn, 1973; Loeb, 1960; Kirk, Osmalov, and Fischer, 1976).

Psychology. The data in Table 3 indicate that psychology editors, relative to sociology editors, have a qualitative emphasis. This is contrary to what I expected. There has been a growing concern among some psychologists that their profession has drifted into a rigorous scientific paradigm. Cedric X (Clark, 1973, p. 6) gives voice to this concern: "One aspect of the value system of American psychology is a recognition that the growth of psychology as a science is inversely related to its frequency of philosophical discussions. Whether this relationship is true or not is of no interest here; the point is that most journal editors believe it to be true."

Sociology. The data in Table 3 suggest that, for sociology, qualitative methodology is underemphasized. Becker (1970) has argued that the strong emphasis on quantitative methodology in sociology is not an accurate reflection of the power of the contributions made using this approach. In fact, Becker suggests that the most important works in sociology have been done by authors using primarily qualitative methods. How can we explain this apparent discrepancy? According to Becker (1970, p. 4), "Beneath this surface diversity, one can easily discern a common pattern: a concern for quantitative methods. . . . Is it too extreme to say that these methodologists would like to turn sociological research into something a machine can do? I think not. . . . Methodologists particularly slight three methods used by prizewinners. They seldom write on participant observation . . . historical analysis . . . and on the knitting together of diverse kinds of research and publicly available material."

Summary.   Cole and Cole (1973) have described the critical function of the stratification system of science. Their evidence from the study of the physical sciences suggests that factors other than scientific and scholarly quality are unimportant in assessing a scientist's work, that a scientist's work, as it moves through the knowledge filtration apparatus of the social stratification system of science, will be primarily judged against the normative criteria of the scientific craft.

My interest has been to outline the elements of the normative criteria. In order to describe the structural relationships between the elements of the normative criteria, I performed an oblique factor analysis on the responses of editors to a checklist inventory of the components of scientific inquiry. From this factor analysis, the two distinctive dimensions of quantitative and qualitative methodological orientation emerged. The analysis further indicated that these dimensions were positively correlated and interlaced by the element of scholarship. To examine further the divergence in emphasis on the normative criteria, I made a cross-disciplinary comparison of the qualitative versus quantitative dimension. The analysis revealed major methodological differences in approaches to knowledge building across the fields.

This chapter has focused on describing the interpretations given by professional journal editorial board members to the normative criteria of the scientific craft. Although it may be stepping on editors' toes a bit to open their interpretations to public scrutiny, it is important for members of the profession to be able to evaluate the technical and artistic norms that regulate knowledge building in the social and behavioral sciences.

4

Organization
and Composition
of Editorial
Review Boards

━━━━━━━━━━━━━━

These editorial board members were selected for their competence. I did not nominate any of my friends and close acquaintances to be associate editors; at the time of the nominations, I had met only two of the nominees, and I had not seen those persons in several years.
—Glenn, 1978, p. 5

One of the more important neglected areas in the sociology of science is the study of the structure and composition of journal editorial boards. Survival and achievement in the academic world require the positive response of journal editorial board members to the presentation of a scientist's manuscripts. Why then is there such a dearth of investigations into this social institution? Perhaps one explanation is that critical examination of editorial boards could leave a sour taste with editors and result in deleterious consequences for the critic's future work. As Clark (1973, p. 5) observes, "To talk about the function of the editor is to make an issue of it, and that is what most editors would like to

avoid. They, like the people they investigate, have self-concep-
tions they would like to retain."

Scientists devote a major part of their academic life to
the task of publishing in professional journals. Publication in
professional journals is a critical factor in determining a scientist's movement within the social stratification system of science
(Hargens, 1975). Publication also allows the scientist to disseminate his or her findings to the public forum of the field. The
mixture of these two motives embraces the concern for publication that attaches to the act of submitting a manuscript for
review by a journal editorial board.

The editorial review board screens manuscripts to filter
out contributions that lack scientific rigor, scholarly quality,
value to the field, or other publishable merit. In the more competitive fields of the social and behavioral sciences, where rejection rates average about 80 percent (Zuckerman and Merton,
1971; American Psychological Association Council of Editors,
1975; Kroll, 1976), the editorial board has the more difficult
task of selecting the best among many high quality contributions.

This *knowledge filtration system* is intimately tied to the
social stratification system of science. The decision to publish
has important consequences not only for the career of the individual whose work is under review but also for the wider reward
and motivation system of science. As Gustin (1973, p. 1131)
remarks, "The charisma of science, embodied in the literature,
is the social cement that enables this cycle of motivation to
function. Indeed the standards of the 'republic of science' function primarily in its defense; the charlatan cannot be tolerated
not merely because his science is technically inadequate, but
because the intrusion of counterfeit into the publication system
would devalue the scientific currency and thus threaten the
legitimacy of the scientific role requirement of publication."

Determination of Quality

In assessing the quality of a submitted manuscript, the
editorial referee employs the normative criteria of the scientific

craft. The data reported in the previous chapter indicated a broad consensus among the editors when identifying these criteria but also revealed a divergence in emphasis of the criteria among the editors and among the different fields. The criterion that recorded the highest overall emphasis among the editors was "value of the author's findings to the field."

There is agreement among the reviewers regarding the criteria against which to judge a manuscript submitted for publication. However, little is known of exactly how the criteria are applied in the review process. Studies of interrater reliability in this judgment process have been discouraging (Scott, 1974; Bowen, Perloff, and Jacoby, 1972). The wide divergence in judgment that results from the application of the criteria may be seen in the following contrasting perspectives of editors:

> I don't think I'm a demanding critic, because I have adopted the rule that if a paper contains at least one good idea and/or some interesting and plausible observation, I am willing to see it in print . . . . It is hard to tell how well I do this, but I have repeatedly recommended papers that bored me but . . . which I thought. . . would interest people in the field.

*   *   *

> One must account for the fact that so much rubbish is published each year in the social sciences (and humanities) and that even more is offered. . . . The innumerable incompetents in the social sciences and the humanities are not deterred by the standards which are exemplified in what is published. Perhaps they are even encouraged by the sight of so much triviality, illiteracy, and dullness to think that what they submit will not fall below the standard. . . . You might have noticed that all papers published in [name of journal] are written in grammatical English and are free of slang and jargon. That is so because I insist on it.

Studies of Interjudge Reliability in the Review Process

In 1971, Bowen, Perloff, and Jacoby collected data on the reliability of judgment among a distinguished group of psychologists. After soliciting sixteen papers for a contest for the best paper submitted to the annual American Psychological Association (APA) convention's Division of Consumer Psychology, the three-person program committee selected the best eight. They then impaneled a group of judges consisting of the past presidents of the division. Each judge independently evaluated and ranked the eight papers. The reliability of this distinguished panel was remarkably low (Kendall's W [coefficient of concordance] was .106 and was not statistically significant). Bowen, Perloff, and Jacoby (1972, p. 221) reported, "Ranges of the ranks assigned to the papers varied greatly. Four of the eight papers were ranked first by at least one judge and eighth by at least one. Ranks of two papers ranged from first to seventh, one from second to eighth, and one from second to seventh." In a similar study, McReynolds (1971) found a range from .21 to .84 on a checklist of criteria for assessing manuscripts. In the most comprehensive study to date, involving 287 double-reviewed manuscripts for the *Journal of Personality and Social Psychology,* Scott (1974) found rather low interclass reliability on a checklist of items assessing a manuscript. Agreement on the double-reviewed manuscripts ranged from .07 to .37 over the seven items included in Scott's rating form (see also Hendrick, 1977).

Reevaluations of published and/or funded research (Ward, Hall, and Schram, 1975; Bernstein and Freeman, 1975) have found a similar imprecision. An evaluation, by a Committee of the American Educational Research Association, of research articles published in 1971 found that "only 8 percent were rated 'acceptable as is for publication,' 31 percent were rated 'acceptable after minor revisions,' 34 percent were rated 'acceptable only after major revisions,' and 27 percent were rated 'reject'" (Ward, Hall, and Schram, 1975, p. 118).

In contrast, Kochen and Perkel (1977, p. 11), in a study of the publication review process at the *Journal of the Association for Computing Machinery*, write, "Our experience has shown that over the past year, of the 'twelve papers reviewed by twenty-four referees, there has been consensus in all but three cases." Since the studies in the social and behavioral sciences have consistently reported an absence of broad consensus, it would appear that the difference is a result of the greater paradigm consensus in the computer field (see Pfeffer, Leong, and Strehl, 1977).

What are the consequences of this low reliability in the social and behavioral sciences? In an intriguing paper, Stinchcombe and Ofshe (1969) constructed a hypothetical model that viewed the editorial reviewing of a journal as a probabilistic process. If, they proposed, one were able to assess the true quality of a manuscript, then, given the current acceptance rate of about 16 percent in the social science journals, the cut point for acceptance would be set for all papers more than 1 standard deviation above the mean. That is, if a measure of the true quality of papers (a hypothetical measure never obtained) was normally distributed, then all papers one standard deviation above the mean (roughly 16 out of 100) would be accepted. However, with the introduction of measurement error into the process of assessing "true quality," not all the best papers would be accepted. Stinchcombe and Ofshe estimate that with a level of reliability equal to .5, half of the best papers on measured "true quality" would be rejected and replaced with papers of lesser quality. Examining a hypothetical sample of 100 papers, they calculated the fate of these papers under a model of .5 reliability (see Table 4). Summarizing their findings, they write (1969, p. 117), "The impressive thing about the model is that it does not take a conspiracy theory of journal editing to account for the rejection of a great many good papers and the publishing of a large number of mediocre papers. Even if social scientists as editors are as accurate as people ever are in coding qualitative material, nearly half the good papers will be rejected and the journals filled with mediocrity."

Yet these reliability data suggest that social and behavioral scientists are *not* as accurate as people ever are. In fact, the studies suggest their level of reliability to be much lower, probably around .2 to .25. In the most rigorous and large-scale study in

TABLE 4. Disposition of 100 Hypothetical Papers Under Two Models of Assessment Reliability.

Interval in Standard Deviations	Expected Number of Papers of True Quality	Model With[a] Reliability of .50		Model With Reliability of .25	
		Expected Acceptances	Expected Rejections	Expected Acceptances	Expected Rejections
-3 to -2	2	0	2	0	2
-2 to -1	14	0	14	1	13
-1 to 0	34	1	33	3	31
0 to +1	34	6	28	6	28
+1 to +2	14	7	7	5	9
+2 to +3	2	2	0	1	1
	100	16	84	16	84

[a]These results assume that the true quality and the observed rating have a bivariate normal distribution with a correlation equal to the square root of the reliability. If ρ^2 is the reliability, the probability of accepting a manuscript whose true quality is X is given by:

$$1 - \Phi[(1 - X\rho)/(\sqrt{1 - \rho^2})]$$

where $\Phi(\cdot)$ is the *cumulative normal distribution function*.

the social and behavioral sciences, Scott (1974) found a range from .07 to .37 for various dimensions of assessment. Using the same probability model as Stinchombe and Ofshe, I computed the rates of acceptance and rejection for a model with .25 reliability (see Table 4). Although this figure is still quite high in view of the studies reviewed earlier, it would be hard to imagine more distressing results. In the revised model, less than one-third of the best papers, measured in units of "true quality," would be accepted. One-fourth of the papers accepted would come from the bottom half of the sample. If the level of reliability slips much below .25 (which is an optimistic figure, in view of empirical studies), all papers have an almost equal likelihood of being accepted.

Why is the level of reliability in assessing manuscripts so low? A variety of explanations have been offered. Stinchcombe and Ofshe (1969) hint at one when they assert that they can explain the current disappointing state of the journal literature without recourse to a conspiracy theory. Yet it is not so much a conspiracy theory that concerns authors (and readers) as it is the possible intrusion of particularistic standards in the review process (Brackbill and Korten, 1970). In a later chapter, this concern will be examined at greater length. Before leaving this issue, however, there is one point that needs discussion.

Pfeffer, Leong, and Strehl (1977) have examined the intrusion of particularistic standards into the review process across several different disciplines. Their study suggests that there is a greater intrusion of particularistic standards in the social and behavioral sciences than in the physical and biological sciences (see Lodahl and Gordon, 1972) and asks what the conditions are for the introduction of particularistic standards. Studies of personnel evaluation and promotion decisions in business and industry, according to Pfeffer, Salancik, and Leblebici (1976), indicate that particularistic standards are used when there is an absence of clear and objective criteria for decision making. With the low level of paradigm consensus in the social and behavioral sciences, the conditions appear to be ideal for the application of particularistic standards.

An illustration of this is provided by a former editor in

chief of a major political science journal. According to the editor, "There are some fields in which there is a very high degree of consensus among reviewers, whereas in others an editor can almost automatically expect major disagreements, especially if the manuscript is sent to representatives of different *schools*." As an example, the editor noted a much higher consensus in the field of American politics (which is fairly quantitative) than in political theory.

For journal editors who need to make a decision regarding a manuscript but are faced with conflicting recommendations from reviewers, the appeal of particularistic standards becomes especially strong. Although this temptation can perhaps be justified as simple use of all available information, it is a clear violation of the norms of science (see Cournand and Meyer, 1976). Since the conditions are so ideal for the introduction of particularistic standards, there is a need for greater vigilance in protecting the manuscript review process.

Designing an Objective Review Mechanism. Because of the low interjudge reliability among reviewers, despite consensus regarding criteria for publication, several writers have recommended that journals use an objective checklist review sheet (containing items similar to those identified in Chapter Three) administered by well-trained clerks (Wolff, 1973). Bowen, Perloff, and Jacoby (1972, pp. 224-225) observe, "One of the major benefits achieved where standardized evaluations have been developed is that relatively unskilled personnel can be trained to produce accurate ratings. . . . Implementation of a more objective technique for assessment of manuscripts just might constitute a major breakthrough toward making the basis of professional recognition more open and less arcane."

There are three major problems with this approach. First, the craft element of science does not lend itself to technical judgments. As Ravetz (1971, p. 274) remarks, "It is impossible to design a simple set of routine tests by which one could assign some numerical marks to a solved scientific problem and then grade it on a linear scale. Nor would it be feasible to erect a formal system of categories of quality and train up corps of expert assessors (such as exist in many other spheres of activity) to operate in their framework. For the techniques are so subtle, the appropriate criteria of adequacy and value so specialized, and the materials so rapidly changing, that any fixed and formalized categories would be a blunt and obsolete instrument as soon as it was brought into use."

Second, the most important criterion in evaluating a manuscript is a judgment of the mauscript's value to the field. This judgment requires a background and experience in the field, which comes from years of active involvement with its issues and problems. On this point, Ravetz (1971, p. 183) observes, "refereeing a paper is a special skill of a mature scientist. It is hardly ever possible to reproduce the data on which the evidence is based, and it is frequently onerous to follow a complex argument through all of its fine structure. So the referee must use his personal knowledge of the craft to form a judgment. For all the referee can assure is that in his judgment the problem is of value and the work adequately performed."

Third, in the current competitive conditions of the social and behavioral sciences, the decision to publish requires the reviewer not only to screen out inadequate work but also to select from among many high-quality manuscripts. The assessment in this situation demands a reviewer with outstanding credentials in research and scholarly inquiry. Without these credentials, the reviewer's judgment would be open to frequent and intensive questioning. On this point, Cole and Cole (1973, pp. 79–80) write, "Given the role that stars play in exercising authority, establishing and maintaining consensus, serving as gatekeepers for scarce resources and as referees for journals, consider what would happen to a field without stars. It is unlikely that a modern science could function at all. Scientists must be found to fill these important positions. If the positions are filled by "average" scientists, it will be difficult for the authority exercised to be granted legitimacy. It is only when the scientific community sees those exercising authority as deserving of it that the authority will be accepted."

In the spring of 1975, I surveyed the editors of the journals included in the cluster sample (see Chapter Three) to determine the criteria they employ in selecting board members. All but three of the eighteen journal editors responded. The most frequently mentioned criteria were the expertise of the candidate and a record of high-quality performance (see Benedik, 1976, for similar findings).

Research Design

Are editorial board members actually characterized by the distinction of their own work and by expertise in their field? To answer this question, I conducted an investigation of the accomplishments of the editorial board members of the cluster sample of journals, collecting data on (1) the number of books, articles, and monographs published; (2) the number of citations these works had received; (3) the place of current employment; (4) the type of current professional assignment; and (5) the highest degree the individual had attained.

Measures. Production measures included locating every article, book, or monograph an editorial board member had published. Articles were located by searching through several abstract services, including *Sociological Abstracts* (1953 [bd] to 1974), *Abstracts for Social Workers* (National Association of Social Workers, 1965 [bd] to 1974), *Psychological Abstracts* (American Psychological Association, 1953 to 1974), *Poverty and Human Resource Abstracts* (Institute of Labor and Industrial Relations, 1967 [bd] to 1974), and several others, as indicated by the editor's specialty (bd is an abbreviation of *beginning date*—when service was initiated). A record was made of each published work, how many authors had contributed to it, and whether the editorial board member was the senior author.

To assess article production, the variable *adjusted total articles* was constructed. This variable consists of the total of all the author's articles after each is divided by the number of authors. No attempt was made to take into account seniority or ranking of authorship. As other investigators have indicated, it is almost· impossible to decompose the relative contribution made by various authors of a paper (Simon, 1970; Zuckerman, 1968).

Books and monographs were located through the 1974 edition of *Books in Print* and *The National Union Catalog* of the Library of Congress (1969, 1973, 1974, 1975). A record was made of each manuscript, the type of manuscript (book, edited book, or monograph), the number of authors, and the edition number. Instead of examining published material individually, all were combined into a weighted measure of total production. The adjustment for multiple authorship involved the same procedure as described above. The weighting of individual items was article (a) = 1, edited book (eb) = 2, book (b) = 5 and manuscript (m) = 1.5. In deciding on these weights, I borrowed from the procedures used by Blau (1973) and Glenn and Villemez (1970). The full equation is thus:

$$production\ index = [\Sigma(a/n) + 5\Sigma\ (b/n) + 2\Sigma\ (eb/n) + 1.5\Sigma\ (m/n)]$$

where n represents the number of authors and the summation is over the years of coverage for the abstract and cataloguing documents.

To determine how often the work of the editorial board member was cited, all of these works, including junior authored productions, were searched in the *Social Science Citation Index* (SSCI) (Institute for Scientific Information, 1970 to 1976). A record was made of each publication cited, keeping account of the number of authors and the year the work was produced. Although the SSCI lists only the first author of a paper, I traced all papers written by an editor irrespective of authorship position. Previous studies that have failed to do this have introduced substantial bias (Lindsey and Staulcup, 1977). I developed from this complete accounting a modified citation measure that incorporated several of the procedures recommended by Myers (1970), such as excluding self-citations, and introduced the adjustment for the number of authors, as explained earlier.

To locate the highest degree the editor had earned and where it was from, I searched the *Comprehensive Dissertation Index, 1861–1972* (Xerox University Microfilms, 1973), supplementing this for several editorial board members who had not earned doctorates with a search of professional directories and author descriptions in published articles (this situation existed only in social work).

Findings

The editorial board members of all the journals report involvement in the review process (see Lindsey, 1976, p. 802). Consequently, the issue here is what qualifications for judgment these editorial board members bring to their task.

Production Counts. The data in Table 5 present the major findings of the survey of the archival sources. The most obvious finding is that social work editorial boards are consistently composed of individuals who, in comparison to the editors in sociology and psychology, are not distinguished by the excellence or volume of their own contribution to the knowledge base of the field. This presents a problem only to the extent that the editorial board members sit at the control panel, so to say, of the scientific enterprise in their respective fields. The underlying question here is, "How is knowledge to be validated in the profession?" I believe the methodology for building, examining, and validating knowledge in social work, as in the other disciplines has to be scientific, and the analysis here begins with this fundamental assumption. (For critical comments on this assumption, see Gilbert, 1977, and Else, 1978.)

Three of the social work journals record median article counts of less than 1. The majority of the members of the editorial boards of these journals have never published an article abstracted by the major abstracting services. In contrast, all of the psychology journals record median article counts above 11. This score is the highest recorded by any of the editorial boards in any of the fields. The sociology boards are also clearly staffed by individuals who have made a substantial contribution to the published literature. We must take into account that social work is a practice profession difficult to compare with the more academically oriented fields of sociology and psychology. In fact, no comparison is intended here. Rather, the primary focus is the structure and composition of editorial boards and their function in the scientific enterprise in the various fields.

Citation Measures. Citation counts have been used by a number of investigators as a rough measure of the impact of an author's published works. The logic is simply that if an author's work is of value it will be used by others. For an assessment of the limitations of this measure, the reader is referred to the Measurement Note at the end of the book.

As knowledge in a given area accumulates, trails are left, in the form of reference citations, to the ongoing work (Chubin, 1973; Line, Sandison, and McGregor, 1972). Concern with the knowledge base in social work, as well as in other fields, has often focused on the cumulative nature of knowledge in the field (Freese, 1972; Kuhn, 1962). The low citation count in social work is disturbing in this regard, for it suggests that social work contributions have resulted in less cumulative knowledge. But there are several difficulties with this suggestion. First, the social work editorial board members in this sample may not be representative of the typical social work scholar or researcher (although one would expect these board members to represent the best scholarship and research in the field). Second, it may be that the knowledge produced in the social work field does not lend itself to use in other fields (compare with Cox, Hamelman, and Wilcox, 1976). For example, there is evidence from the field of business and economics that contributions made by economic theorists are more often used by specialists in marketing than vice versa (Hamelman and Mazze, 1973). This lack of utility to other fields could suggest that although social workers frequently cite the work of sociologists and psychologists, the citation patterns is not reciprocal (the data in Chapter Six, Table 19, support this lack of utility).

Of course, one factor here may be, again, the nature of differing professional enterprises. An illustration is provided in the case of engineering and science. Price (1969) studied the development of both the natural sciences and technology by tracing the pattern of citations among scientific papers. Fores (1971) has been critical of Price's work for not taking into consideration the distinctive character of both science and technology. In this regard, Fores argues that Price's "paper model" has proven instructive in studying science but falls short of the

TABLE 5. Median Measures of Production and Quality of Contribution to Knowledge for Journal Editorial Board Members in Psychology, Social Work, and Sociology.

Journal	n	Adjusted Total Articles	Production Index	Adjusted Total Citations	Percent Doctoral Degree	Corrected Quality Ratio
Psychology						
Journal of Abnormal Psychology	20	12.8	21.3	39.5	100	58.0
Journal of Applied Psychology	21	15.8	21.3	68.5	100	73.5
Journal of Counseling Psychology	26	11.1	19.1	10.8	100	11.4
Journal of Educational Psychology	15	20.8	22.8	41.0	100	75.8
Journal of Personality and Social Psychology	19	12.6	20.9	59.5	100	90.9
Total	101	13.0	21.0	39.3	100	50.1
Social Work						
Child Welfare[a]	10	0.1	0.1	0.1	20	0.06
Clinical Social Work Journal	17	2.4	4.5	3.3	41	2.65
Journal of Education for Social Work	19	1.1	2.0	0.9	74	0.47
Social Casework	14	0.9	1.0	0.8	36	0.68

editorial board member's manuscript has attracted. For instance, if a board member has published (as was true in this sample) more than ten articles and several books and yet attracted no citations, there is reason to suspect the usefulness of his or her work. In contrast, if a board member published five papers that attracted more than fifty citations a year, then there is reason to believe that this work is of high quality. Social work editorial boards had the lowest relative showing on the adjusted measure of the citations-to-production ratio. In contrast, the psychology editorial board members recorded the highest scores. The scores of the sociology editorial boards were also quite high.

The data reviewed here consistently suggest that the individuals selected for editorial board membership in psychology and sociology have achieved scientific distinction. This finding is important for the knowledge construction enterprise in these fields, because the editorial board members make the decisions on what contributions should be added to the knowledge base.

Social Work. The social work editorial boards consistently record low relative scores on all of the measures used here. This can be attributed to a variety of causes. One explanation may be that, while the editorial boards in sociology and psychology are dominated by university-based professionals (87 percent for psychology and 94 percent for sociology), those in social work constitute only 59 percent of that sample. Of social work editors, 41 percent are in government or private settings, where publication is less of a requirement. A similar pattern has been observed in education by Silverman (1976, p. 483), who writes, "Certainly, editors of some research journals are chosen by colleagues on the basis of reputation in a scholarly association—reputation based on productivity as well as informal ties to influentials. However, this pattern does not hold for most editors of education journals who are employed by educational associations, deans of colleges, or entrepreneurs."

Most of the nonuniversity professionals on the social work editorial boards hold administrative positions. These administrators record a surprisingly low performance on all the measures of contributions to knowledge used here (see Table 6).

Another unique feature of the social work editorial boards

TABLE 6. Mean Adjusted Total Citation Count
by Title of Position and Area.

Title of Position	Sociology	Social Work	Psychology	Citations
Assistant Professor	7	12	2	8.33
Associate Professor	24	12	11	23.35
Full Professor [a]	67	29	76	57.19
Administrator [b]	0	34	1	2.29
Researcher	6	0	12	20.37
Direct Service	0	5	2	4.27
Totals	104	92	104	

NOTE: N = 300

[a] Several of the full professors held concurrent positions as deans or department chairpersons, which are administrative positions. The categorization utilized here was selected in the interest of maintaining the university-nonuniversity break while elaborating by positions held.
[b] Citations of administrators include only social work administrators.

is the presence of nondoctorate professionals. None of the board members of the sociology and psychology journals was without a doctorate. Inspection of Table 5 reveals, however, that the *Clinical Social Work Journal*, even though it has a low percentage of doctorates on its editorial board, had one of the highest scores on citation and production measures. Several of the other boards reflect the same inconsistent pattern.

The Function of Professional Journals in Social Work

The underlying assumption here is that the professional journals serve primarily to publish, distribute, and store in the knowledge archives of the discipline the results of scientific and scholarly inquiry. Disagreeing with this assumption, Feinstein (personal communication, November 1975) writes, "The goal of a journal is to provide articles to increase the flow of information between the researcher and the human services practitioner . . . . In our opinion, persons with significant experience and distinguished achievement in the administration, planning, and delivery of human service programs are excellent judges of what material is useful to practitioners and what is not." In addition, Gilbert (1977, p. 1109) remarks, "First, it is debatable whether comparisons of distinction and achievement between board members of journals serving a profession and those serving academic disciplines should be conceptualized along the exact same dimensions, that is, publication. [This approach] denies other forms of distinction that would attest to a reviewer's competence and talent to make sound judgments about professional journal manuscripts."

All professional journals provide for the dissemination of knowledge. The journal literature becomes, in this manner, the depository for the knowledge base of the disciplines. The specific discrepancy here concerns the type of knowledge the journals select for dissemination. In the fields of psychology and sociology, the professional journals serve to evaluate the scientific and scholarly merit of manuscripts. The concern of the journals in these two fields is to communicate scientific and scholarly developments to professional audiences. In social work, several journals have adopted a remedial and/or continuing education function, their concern being to present popularized discussions of current issues. As Schoenberg (personal communication, November 1975) writes, "Our Publications Advisory Committee . . . merely helps us with advice on how to get *Child Welfare* read by more persons in the child welfare field, most of whom are untrained and now read little or nothing of a professional nature."

The function of dispensing basic information in a readable format has traditionally been the responsiblity of textbooks. If social work journals take on this task, it will not be without sacrificing the larger effort of constructing a cumulative knowledge base for the profession. In this regard, Flexner's advice in 1915 (p. 590) is still appropriate: "A profession must find a dignified and critical means of expressing itself in the form of a periodical, which shall describe in careful terms whatever work is in progress; and it must from time to time register its more impressive performances in a literature of growing solidity and variety. To some extent, the evolution of social work toward the professional status can be measured by the quality of publications put forth in its name."

Conclusion

The primary social institution responsible for processing and evaluating contributions to knowledge is the professional journal. The editorial review board of the professional journal confers authority and legitimacy on contributions to knowledge by selecting only a few for publication. The editorial board members of professional journals have the demanding task of reviewing the large number of submitted manuscripts, and their decisions are critical to the validation and construction of a knowledge base in the social and behavioral sciences. The data reported here indicate that the journal editorial boards in psychology and sociology are staffed by scientists having a high level of distinction. However, the data consistently indicate that the editorial boards in social work are not staffed by scientists of comparable distinction.

As a consequence, the material selected for inclusion in the social work knowledge archives may not be representative of the highest quality of scholarly and research work submitted. To the extent that this interpretation is valid, the social work profession, with its concomitant knowledge base, is restricted in two critical respects. First, the social stratification system in social work is deprived of its full measure of legitimacy and authority. As a result, the ability of the profession to motivate and reward high-quality scholarly and research effort is diminished. Second, the knowledge archives of social work may be cluttered with the debris of merely entertaining and administratively palatable publications.

5

Dynamics of the Publication Decision-Making Process

━━━━━━━━━━━━━━━━━━━

*While serving central roles in focusing issues and devel-
oping the professional literature, editors are frequently
marginal men for whom the maintenance of influence
through position strongly suggests the advisability of
strengthening the established order rather than questioning its roots and advocating radical ideas. A periodic
critical article appears but is like the bite of a mosquito
on an elephant; although such articles are published by
editors, they seem to support the image of academic
freedom rather than its conscious use.*
—Silverman, 1976, p. 484

Most journal editorial boards are staffed by scientists of distinction. Yet in many cases the primary reason for creating an
editorial board is to include on the masthead of a journal the
names of the most distinguished scientists in a particular area.
Such a staffing policy leads to editorial boards with a veneer of
distinction and authority. But, as Crandall (1977) has asked,

who among this select group of eminent scientists (many of whom are undoubtedly immersed in their own research) actually does the work of editorial review?

If individuals of eminence actually guard the gates, the current condition of the social and behavioral sciences is even more perplexing. How is it that so much that is trivial, unintelligently written, illogically argued, erroneous, or incoherent is published yearly? Of what value are these venerable editorial board members who say that they are watchful when, in fact, they abandon their posts to lesser colleagues most of the time? These questions point to the limitations of the analysis of staffing patterns (Chapter Four) and to the need for an examination of the actual process of manuscript review by editorial board members.

It is difficult to examine the review process, because it is subjective and confidential. Objective measures of the activities of the editorial review board are not available. Several studies have examined the possible intrusion of nonscientific criteria into the review process (Crane, 1965; Mahoney, Kazdin, and Kenigsberg, 1978), but the findings have been inconclusive.

It is impossible to map out, isolate, and control the wide variety of influences impinging on editorial decision making. The question must, therefore, be approached indirectly. In this chapter, I take a unique line of inquiry, with several indexes derived for the most part from publicly available data.

Eminence and Editorial Influence

Examination of archival data indicated that editorial board members, at least in psychology and sociology, are characterized by scientific achievement. According to the self-reports of editors, board members are primarily appointed on the basis of their expertise and distinction (see Benedik, 1976). Nevertheless, there is a variation of influence on the review process among editorial board members. Not all board members review the same number of manuscripts, nor positively recommend the same percentage of those reviewed, nor have the same percentage of journal concurrence with their recommendations (see Lindsey, 1976, p. 801). Can variations in editorial influence be correlated to variations in scientific achievement?

Before addressing this question, it was first necessary to develop a measure of editorial power. This is a difficult problem, for which I shall offer an initial, albeit limited, solution. With a measure of editorial influence operationalized, it will then be possible to perform a regression analysis to determine the factors that account for the variation in editorial power among the journal board members.

Editorial Power

To set an initial measure of editorial influence, I defined *editorial power* as the number of manuscripts a board member reviews, taking into account the frequency with which he or she recommends positively and the percentage of times his or her journal concurs with the recommendation. The journal editorial board members in the cluster sample were asked the following questions to determine their editorial power:

1. About how many articles did you review last year?
2. Approximately what percentage of these did you finally recommend for publication?
3. About what percentage of your suggestions for publication was followed by the journal?

With the response to these questions, an index was constructed of the number of articles a reviewer was able to assist toward publication:

$$editorial\ power = n \times r \times c$$

where n represents the number of articles reviewed during the year, r represents the percentage of manuscripts recommended for publication, and c represents the percentage of times the journal concurred with the reviewer's recommendation.

Before proceeding with the analysis, several comments

about this measure are in order. To begin with, it may be objected that this index, by multiplying the number of manuscripts reviewed by the percentage positively recommended, inflates the score of easy reviewers and deflates the score of more rigorous reviewers. This criticism rests on the normative assumption that more rigorous reviewers should not have their measured influence reduced by the lower percentage of positive recommendations. The validity of the editorial power index, as it is used here, does not rest on this normative assumption. The editorial power measure is an empirical index of an editorial board member's ability to assist manuscripts toward publication.

The organizational apparatus that should correct for this possible inflation (or deflation) of editorial power is the office of the editor. Since most of the board members have had review experience and are well known by their editors, the inflated (or deflated) rate of positive recommendations should be corrected by the rate of journal concurrence (both of which are included in the index).

Another limitation of the index of editorial power is that it does not directly assess the ability to make negative evaluations stick. In this sense, the index is not adequately sensitive to the intellectual control function served by editorial review boards. As Solomon (personal communication, February 1976) has pointed out, "Gatekeepers fulfill their role just as well by slamming the gate in people's faces as by letting them through. That is, editorial power involves the ability of board members to make their negative opinions stick, with respect to final publication, as well as positive ones." Blalock has commented in a personal communication (March 1976), "A reviewer who says 'no' to virtually every manuscript does have an important kind of power, namely veto power. I rather suspect, although have no data on it, that standards vary by subfield. Sometimes "methodologists' play the dirty role of being used to reject a relatively high proportion of manuscripts which might seem interchangeable in terms of substantive merit. For example, how can the editor of a very general journal such as the *ASR* really make a judgment on the substantive merits of papers in fields in which he/she does not know the literature? But there are methodological grounds, and perhaps this is one reason why they may get weighted heavily—they crosscut the substantive areas." One way to include this control function would be to equate editorial power with the product of the *number of manuscripts reviewed* and the *journal concurrence rate*. The path analysis to be discussed later permits an indirect examination of this alternative.

The index has several other limitations. First, there is an implicit assumption that all manuscripts distributed to the board members are of equal quality (or at least are randomly distributed). The differential distribution of manuscripts by the editor on the dimension of quality is only partially assessed by the index. Second, the publication review proceedings is a group process, with most editors using several reviewers for each manuscript. The publication decision often reflects several conflicting recommendations (see the discussion in Chapter Four of interjudge reliability in the review process). I have no measure of this interaction effect in the final review decision of the journal.

Third, most journals use reviewers from outside of the editorial board, whose influence may be as important as the board members'. The sample frame for this data set does not include representation of outside reviewers. With these limitations in view, it should still prove instructive to examine the editorial review process with the editorial power index.

Normative theory in the field of the sociology of science proposes that a scientist's work ought to be judged primarily for its scientific merit by universalistic standards as it moves through the screening apparatus of the social stratification system of science (Merton, 1957; Parsons, 1951). My concern here is to examine data that provide an indirect empirical test of the normative theory as it applies to the scientific enterprise in psychology, social work, and sociology. Within this broad theoretical concern, the specific task is to identify and assess those factors that provide the best prediction of the degree of influence an editorial board member exercises in the manuscript review process.

To assess that influence, a regression analysis was performed on the editorial power index. The independent variables in the analysis were the same measures of production and citations discussed in Chapter Four, factor scores of qualitative and quantitative orientation (as discussed in Chapter Three), and prestige measures of the board member's doctorate and place of current employment (Roose and Andersen, 1970).

Two of the independent variables in the analysis do not conform to the strict requirements of regression analysis (Harris, 1975)—ordinal measures of prestige of doctorate and prestige of employment. In accordance with the procedures for mixed systems (such as ordinal- and interval-level measures) recommended by Smith (1974), the cross-level measurement statistics were calculated for introduction into the regression analysis. To control for curvilinearity, two of the independent variables (production and citations) and the dependent variable were log (base 10) transformed (Edwards, 1976).

In the previous chapters, I examined psychology, social work, and sociology simultaneously. However, because social work required the use of different variables in the analysis of editorial power, I will return to it after examining psychology and sociology. Data from psychology and sociology were initally examined together, but as the analysis proceeded it became clear, in light of the substantial differences found between these two disciplines, that they needed to be examined separately.

Psychology

The data in Table 7 display the beta weights that resulted from the regression analysis of the independent variables on editorial power. The zero-order coefficients are displayed along with the standardized regression coefficients (beta weights) in order to permit an exploration of causal structures.

The beta weights are not fully consistent with the proposition that measures of the volume and quality of scientific work best predict the degree of influence an editorial board member will exercise in the review process. In fact, there is an opposite dual influence of these measures. Production records a strong positive impact on editorial power. This is reasonable. What is perplexing is that citations have a strong negative effect

TABLE 7.   Determinants of Editorial Power for Psychology Journals.

	Beta Weight	Zero-Order Correlation
Origin of Doctorate	.036	.109
Production	.406[a]	.032
Quantitative Orientation	.238[a]	.243
Present Employment	.019	.044
Citations	-.456[a]	-.214

NOTE: N = 81; editors were not included in this and subsequent tables since, while presumably they were responsible for at least a brief review of all articles, they did not specifically review any articles involved in these data.

[a] More than three times the standard error.

on editorial power; this means that the more citations a board member has, the less influence he or she is likely to exercise, all other things being equal. This finding is contrary to what the normative model of science would predict.

Comparing the beta weights to the zero-order coefficients reveals a conjoint influence of citations and production on editorial power (Rosenberg, 1968). The zero-order coefficients indicate that production is not correlated with editorial power, while citations have a small negative correlation. However, when production and citations are examined conjointly in the regression analysis, an emergent influence is revealed. Production exerts a strong positive influence, while citations exert an even greater negative impact on editorial power.

The emergent conjoint influence of production and citations on editorial power is quite astonishing, for it suggests that if one wanted to estimate the influence of a particular editorial board member, the best predictor would be citations—negatively weighted! Since citations have been used as a rough measure of the quality of an individual's work, it would be expected that the influence would be in the opposite direction.

In order more carefully to explore the network of influence of the independent variables on editorial power, a path analysis was computed (Blalock, 1971, pp. 73–151; Duncan, 1975). The path analysis allows for the tracing out of the paths through which the independent variables exert their influence on the dependent variable. Path-analytic models are not without serious shortcomings, especially when ordinal variables are introduced (Lazarsfeld, 1975; Wilson, 1974; Leik, 1976). My own view in this regard is similar to Blalock's (1975, pp. 227-228) summary: "The approach I recommend is to think in terms of causal laws expressable as equations requiring metric information, see what these imply in terms of a set of weak tests with ordinal measures, and use the insights obtained to sharpen theoretical models and find ways to obtain more precise measures whenever practicable."

One problem with the regression analysis is the use of a composite index to measure the dependent variable. Following the suggestion of both Duncan (1966) and Solomon (personal communication, February 1976), the dependent variable was decomposed. The path diagram for the psychology editorial board members is shown in Figure 1 (for a decomposition of the dependent variable in terms of the component parts, see Lindsey, 1977a, p. 582).

The path diagram conforms to much of the earlier regression analysis. Production exerts a moderate direct influence on both the number of papers reviewed and the suggest for publication rate. Citations have a moderate, direct, negative influence on both these same components of editorial power. One possible interpretation of this unexpected finding is that the conjoint influence of these independent variables reveal typological influences. The eminent scholar, characterized by a high citation count, independent of production volume, is awarded a seat on the editorial board only to increase the prestige of the journal but participates minimally in the review process. Blalock (personal communication, March 1976) provides a personal illustration: "Journals vary considerably in their prestige and degree to which they are "established." It has been my experience that unestablished ones ... tend to rely on at least some "figureheads" to whom they send virtually no manuscripts. In fact, they may almost guarantee this when they invite the person—who may be inclined to say no because of commitments. I'm on two boards

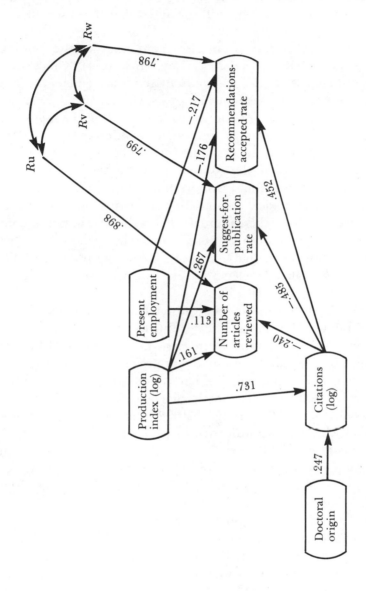

FIGURE 1. Path Diagram of the Determinants of Editorial Power for Psychology Journals.

of foreign journals and two methodological ones that are of this type. In the case of the latter two, I've asked to get off but have been urged to stay on, with the agreement that I would get only an occasional manuscript."

The interpretation also conforms to the findings of Kochen and Perkel (1977). They write (p. 4) "Our experience has shown that to a large extent the more eminent a judge is, the less time he seems willing to spend reviewing manuscripts. The younger, less well-known readers are often the most prompt, conscientious, thorough, and objective referees."

In contrast to the eminent scholar is the high producer, the workhorse of the journal review enterprise, who reviews more manuscripts and is more likely to recommend favorably. This is a paradoxical combination of features in view of the high rejection rates of these journals. The eminent scholar, in contrast, appears to be more rigorous in the review proceeding (or to be more control oriented), further diminishing the small influence he or she already elects to exercise in assisting manuscripts toward print.

The editor or the journal board could exercise some restraint on these paradoxical influences of citations and production. Obviously, just the reverse influence would be desired. That is, it would be normatively desirable if citations recorded a substantial positive influence and production a moderate reverse influence. The path diagram indicates the desired reversal. There is a strong positive influence of citations and a moderate negative influence of production on the *journal concurrence rate*. In the process of evaluating a referee's recommendation for publication, the psychology editors appear to take into account the referee's own scientific efforts as these are reflected in citations.

If a screening process occurs before a manuscript is sent out for review, the editor may send the best manuscripts to the most eminent judges. If this were true, it would indicate that the first-rate papers, which are sent to the more eminent judges, are more critically scrutinized and thus less likely to be accepted for publication.

TABLE 8.   Determinants of Editorial Power for Sociology Journals.

	Beta Weight	Zero-Order Correlation
Origin of doctorate	.216[a]	.170
Production	.006	.080
Quantitative orientation	.112	.032
Present employment	.110	.078
Citations	.140	.111

NOTE: N = 79.
[a] More than three times the standard error.

Sociology

With the sociology journals, as with the data for the psychology journals, the standardized coefficients for the independent variables are not consistent with expectations (see Table 8). However, the patterns of deviation from the normative science model is different than that found for the psychology journals. The measure of production has almost no influence. The citation measure records only a small influence. None of the standardized coefficients is particularly large (only one is statistically signficant). This suggests either that other variables have been left out of the analytic model or that there is limited systematic variance.* Since several of these same variables were useful in estimating editorial power among psychology editorial board members, the latter explanation becomes less tenable.

Perhaps the most important source of variance from unobserved variables operating here comes from those whom Zuckerman (1970, p. 239) describes as the second echelon of scientists, "those who contribute to the ongoing operation of

*Within the path-analytic framework, this problem of measurement error takes on increased importance (see Blalock, 1964; Allison, 1976). Measurements either of production or of citations that fail to consider multiple authorship may introduce considerable measurement error (see Lindsey and Staulcup, 1977). When production and citations are treated as intervening variables, as is often the case (Cole and Cole, 1973; Lightfield, 1971), this error frequently exceeds reasonable levels of tolerance. The measures of production and citations used throughout this book control for multiple authorship.

their fields by taking on the demanding administrative and editorial tasks. Their influence derives from their positions rather than from the personal authority of having done significant scientific work. They have probably accepted the fact that they will not do pathbreaking research but they have good enough scientific taste and sufficient energies to do useful work as participants in disciplinary politics." Since scientific taste is not an objective matter, it has not been possible to include it as an observed variable. It might be useful in future research to develop an index of "editorial work habits" and determine the influence of this factor on editorial power. Obviously, editorial reviewers who eagerly and efficiently execute their review assignments can be expected to have greater editorial power (Rodman, 1970; McCartney, 1978).

The variable that recorded the greatest influence in the estimation equation for editorial power was the prestige measure of doctoral origin. This is quite contrary to what the normative model of science would suggest but is consistent with earlier studies by Yoels (1971, 1974) indicating that the origin of the doctorate was a useful variable in predicting the appointment patterns to social science journals.

The path diagram in Figure 2 provides a graphic illustration of how the independent variables exert their influence on the dependent variable (see Lindsey, 1977a, p. 583, for a decomposition of the dependent variable). Production has a small direct negative influence on the number of articles reviewed component of the variable. In contrast to the path diagram for psychology, citations exhibit a substantial positive influence on the number of articles reviewed. The conjoint emergent influence that characterized the psychology journals does not hold for the sociology journals. Rather, just the reverse characterizes the network of influence. This would indicate less concern in sociology with the prestige the appointment of a board member brings to the journal. Instead, the concern is with obtaining assistance in the manuscript review process. One explanation of this may be the shorter appointment time for board members and editors in sociology.

The data for both the psychology and sociology editorial

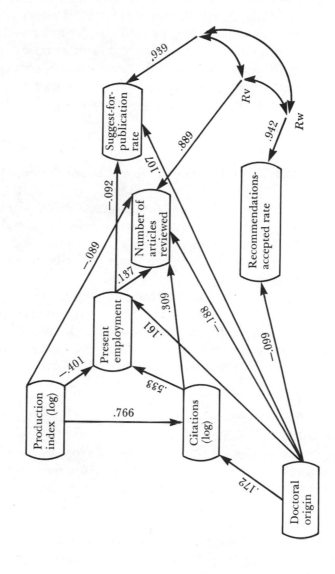

FIGURE 2. Path Diagram of the Determinants of Editorial Power for Sociology Journals.

board members indicate that it is quite difficult to explain participation and influence in the publication review process with the normative model of science. The variables that the investigators from the normative tradition have identified as important (Cole and Cole, 1973; Reskin, 1976, 1977) either account for an insignificant amount of explained variance or have a significant opposite influence. Because the publication review process is fundamental to the social stratification system of science (Gustin, 1973; Zuckerman and Merton, 1971), the failure of the normative model here raises serious concern regarding its general usefulness.

Revised Measures of Editorial Board Distinction

In Chapter Four, we found substantially higher median scores for the editors of psychology journals on several measures of scientific achievement. The data are reproduced in Table 9 with a shift to mean scores in order to facilitate a subsequent analytic procedure.

The preceding analysis suggests that psychology journals appoint a number of eminent scholars who serve as figureheads to enhance the prestige of the journal but who do not participate in the manuscript review process. In sociology, eminent contributors and high producers apparently share in the review proceedings, with the eminent contributors exercising the greater influence.

To determine if, in fact, there is a difference in the measures of production and citations of the board members when the degree of influence in the editorial review process is taken into account, weighted values of the measures in Table 9 were calculated. The revised measures in Table 10 represent the mean scores on the measures when the individual board members' scores have each been weighted by their respective editorial power scores. The revised measures indicate the characteristics of the typical manuscript reviewer, rather than board member, for the respective journals. The results reveal a greater similarity between the two fields on measures of scientific

TABLE 9. Measures of Production and Quality of Contribution to Knowledge for Journal Editorial Board Members in Psychology and Sociology

	Adjusted Total Articles	Production Index	Adjusted Total Citations	Corrected Quality Ratio
Psychology Journals				
Journal of Abnormal Psychology	15.8	21.9	52.7	82.9
Journal of Applied Psychology	19.9	29.3	84.0	157.8
Journal of Counseling Psychology	27.6	39.7	49.4	47.8
Journal of Educational Psychology	20.5	28.7	88.8	126.7
Journal of Personality and Social Psychology	15.6	21.0	80.5	184.2
Total	18.8	27.1	60.6	94.0
Sociology Journals				
American Sociologist	7.0	13.3	38.6	65.3
American Sociological Review	12.7	21.3	52.6	90.7
Journal of Health and Social Behavior	14.5	21.3	39.7	52.3
Sociology of Education	8.4	14.2	37.1	49.1
Social Forces	10.3	16.9	28.8	35.7
Social Problems	11.5	18.8	43.5	66.3
Total	11.3	18.8	43.5	64.6

NOTE: Values displayed are mean scores for measures. Mean is preferable to median when computing weighted values.

TABLE 10. Measures of Production and Quality of Contribution to Knowledge Adjusted for Editorial Power for Board Members in Psychology and Sociology

	Adjusted Total Articles	Production Index	Adjusted Total Citations	Corrected Quality Ratio
Psychology Journals				
Journal of Abnormal Psychology	17.7	23.4	58.5	92.4
Journal of Applied Psychology	18.1	26.8	57.1	83.3
Journal of Counseling Psychology	13.6	19.9	23.6	25.7
Journal of Educational Psychology	17.6	24.0	55.5	82.9
Journal of Personality and Social Psychology	13.8	22.0	73.2	133.5
Total	15.3	22.0	40.6	55.2
Sociology Journals				
American Sociologist	7.9	12.8	47.5	91.5
American Sociological Review	12.1	20.2	51.8	83.0
Journal of Health and Social Behavior	21.7	31.1	79.5	127.1
Sociology of Education	8.2	15.6	52.7	96.9
Social Forces	14.1	21.6	41.1	56.7
Social Problems	11.4	18.3	46.8	74.8
Total	14.4	22.3	57.1	91.4

NOTE: Values displayed are mean scores for measures. Mean is preferable to median when computing weighted values.

achievement among editorial boards when the factor of actual involvement in the editorial review process is brought into consideration.

Social Work

As earlier discussion indicated, social work journals operate in a fashion quite different from those in other fields. Several variables not useful in the analysis of the editorial review process in psychology or sociology emerged as quite useful, even essential, to the analysis in social work. Foremost among these were measures of institutional prestige and possession of the doctorate. Since a large number of board members in social work were not affiliated with universities (see Table 6), it became necessary to construct a new measure. The measure that seemed most meaningful and proved most useful was a dichotomous variable of university affiliation (that is, university based versus not university based). Similarly, since many of the board members in social work did not have a doctorate, it was necessary to use a dichotomous measure for the possession of a doctorate. The last additional variable was a dichotomous measure of whether the board member held an administrative position. A large number of editorial board members of social work journals were administrators (see Table 6). This variable emerges as quite important in understanding social work editorial board decisions.

Table 11 shows the beta weights that resulted from the regression analysis with the new variables for social work entered into the equation. The beta weights from the analysis are again inconsistent with the proposition, from the normative theory of science, that measures of the volume and appeal of scientific work determine the degree of influence an editorial board member exercises in the review process. The most influential variable here is university affiliation.

The second most influential variable was the qualitative orientation of the individual board member. This is consistent with the finding that editors in social work show a greater

TABLE 11. Determinants of Editorial Power for Social Work Journals.

	Beta Weight	Simple Correlation
Administrator	.201	−.323
University based	.453	.458
Doctorate	−.040	.313
Production index	.319	.394
Citations	.064	.297
Qualitative orientation	.368	.415

NOTE: R^2 = .39.

qualitative emphasis than those in other disciplines (see Table 3). The fact that qualitative orientation exerts such a strong independent influence perhaps suggests an unwarranted bias (in the next chapter, the consequences of this bias will be discussed). There is a moderate zero-order correlation between editorial power and the possession of an earned doctorate, but when other variables are controlled this influence is diminished. Thus the possession of a doctorate exerts its influence on editorial power indirectly. Controlling other variables, the quantity of published work exerts a moderate positive influence. Thus production, regardless of citations, results in greater influence in the editorial review proceedings. Although administrative status exhibits a moderate negative influence as a simple correlation, when other variables are controlled it records a small positive influence. Thus administrative status appears to exert a strong independent influence. The shift in influence between the beta-weight and the zero-order correlations for administrative status, possession of the doctorate, and citations highlights the need to examine more carefully the network of influence among the independent and dependent variables (Lyons, 1971).

The path diagram in Figure 3 conforms to much of the earlier regression analysis (see Lindsey, 1978, for the decomposition of the dependent variable). Production exerts a small direct influence on both the number of articles reviewed and the suggest for publication rate. However, production exerts its strongest direct influence on the journal concurrence rate. This is an odd place for this variable to exert influence and certainly

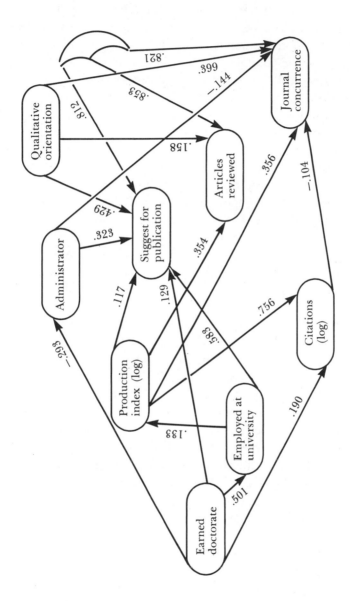

FIGURE 3. Path Diagram of the Determinants of Editorial Power in Social Work Journals.

not in conformity with the analysis for psychology and sociology. It would make more sense for this variable to be influential at the beginning rather than the end of the review process. If its influence is at the beginning, it suggests that productive individuals receive more editorial assignments. Coming at both the end and the beginning of the review process, it suggests that productive social work authors not only are reviewing more manuscripts but also are listened to with greater respect in the final decision.

In contrast to production, citations exert only a small negative impact on the journal concurrence rate. This would suggest that the journals are responsive to visible evidence of production (the number of papers published) but not to the recognition of those papers as reflected by citations.

The influence of an administrative position on editorial power is transmitted through a higher rate of favorable suggestion for publication. Likewise, the university affiliation registers its influence directly on the rate of favorable recommendations. Thus, controlling the other factors associated with university affiliation (such as production and citations), there is a substantial direct influence toward higher rates of journal concurrence. The similar influence of these dissimilar (almost opposite) variables demonstrates the powerful indirect effect of the other variables.

The qualitative orientation factor score transmits its influence through moderately positive paths to both suggest for publication rates and recommendations accepted rates. This indicates that the qualitative bias of social work editorial boards does not emerge until the second stage of the review process, after submitted mansucripts have been distributed to reviewers. However, a small positive influence of qualitative orientation on the number of articles reviewed tempers the preceding statement, indicating the possibility of this bias affecting all stages of the review process.

The data indicate the limited usefulness of normative theory in accurately predicting the operations of editorial boards in this field. The citations rate, which should, according to theory, be of primary influence, has only a small positive influence. For social work, instead of universalistic criteria being primary, a strong qualitative bias prevails.

The positive influence of production on the components of editorial power suggests that influence in the publication review proceeding increases with measures of scientific contribution to the field. To determine if there is a change in the measures of production and citations among the editorial board members when editorial power is taken into account, I used the approach followed with the sociology and psychology editorial boards. Weighted values of citations and production measures are reported in Table 12. These revised measures represent the median scores when the cases are weighted by the editorial power score. The median index of central location was retained for this subsample because of its robustness with small counts (Mosteller and Tukey, 1977). The results indicate that the social work editorial boards as a whole make use of the best talent available to them. That is, when editorial influence is taken into consideration, the production and citation measures consistently increase for the journals as a whole.

When the journals are examined individually, the data indicate that some of the boards make better use of available talent. For example, *Social Work* increases by almost threefold its score on measures of production and citations when editorial power is taken into account. In contrast, the *Journal of Education for Social Work* and *Social Service Review* both record reductions. It appears that most of the overall increase on these measures came about as a result of the journal *Social Work*. Since *Social Work* appoints board members partly to achieve regional, sexual, racial, and religious balance, we may ask whether such appointments result in different review decisions for the journal. As one board member replied on the questionnaire, "I have reviewed so few papers [none for the year] that I suspect I am being ignored. This questionnaire reminds me that I should resign."

Discussion. The data on the publication review process among the major journals in social work indicate a strong bias in favor of qualitative methods of building knowledge. This bias partly reflects the powerful humanistic current that runs

TABLE 12. Median Measures of Production and Quality of Contribution to Knowledge Adjusted for Editorial Power for Board Members in Social Work.

	Adjusted Total Articles	Production Index	Adjusted Total Citations	Corrected Quality Ratio
Child Welfare	0	0	0.2	0
Clinical Social Work Journal	2.3	6.9	3.4	2.71
Journal of Education for Social Work	0.8	1.5	0.2	0.01
Social Casework	1.3	1.3	1.3	2.00
Social Work	6.3	6.9	6.2	5.90
Social Service Review	5.2	3.4	5.3	4.33
Urban and Social Change Review	0.1	0.1	0.2	0.14
Total	3.0	4.3	2.1	2.19

throughout the social work profession. However, the qualitative bias can at times be antithetical to the quantitative spirit of science. Several studies have found a major resistance to empirical research in the practice settings of social work. This resistance is reflected by the editorial board members examined in this study.

Except for one or two journals, editorial boards control the major social work journals with a view toward remedial education, entertainment, and wide circulation rather than knowledge building (see Chapter Four). The editorial boards of social work journals are not comparable in scientific distinction to the editorial boards in other fields. Even though several of the journals seem aware of this fact and overutilize their scholarly and scientific members, this is a limited compensatory approach. What is needed is a policy on the appointment of review board members that takes into consideration the knowledge building function of the professional journals. There are indications that this situation is changing (see Else, 1978; Lindsey, 1977b).

The findings reported here may be taken as harshly critical of the social work profession. Yet the focus of this analysis has not been the profession as a whole, with whose contribution to a more humane and improved social condition I proudly identify myself. Rather, the critical analysis has been directed toward the composition and administration of editorial review boards in social work.

The social work editorial boards exercise a tremendous influence on the profession. Their decisions have effects that are felt throughout the profession, in the literature, and among potential contributors, and ripple on down to the clients served. How is respect to be acquired, if it is not earned? Why do the innumerable individuals who have been appointed to social work editorial boards, who have never published a paper themselves that was abstracted by a major abstracting service, have the privilege of deciding what should be published and what should not? These individuals occupy highly desired and sought-after positions. It is unclear why they, and not others, were appointed. They are marginal contributors to the literature they serve to guard. As marginal individuals, they are beholden to their appointers—to those who have, so to say, turned the clay into sculpture. As a consequence, we confront a condition where a great deal of substandard work appears in the social work literature. I am not arguing against the value of practice literature or program description. Rather, I am opposed to individuals passing judgment who have not earned that privilege through their own merit but have instead had it bestowed on them. If the social work journals are to appoint board members on a fair or honest or competitive basis, then the criteria for appointment should be spelled out and adherence to the criteria demonstrated; otherwise I am left with a nagging feeling that something is amiss.

Some of the results reported here regarding social work journal editorial boards have been reported previously. I feel uncomfortable with the way in which at least one critic (Gilbert, 1977) and perhaps others have read my research. It might help clear the air a little if I discuss the assumptions and concerns that have motivated this investigation.

In my research, I have operated on the assumption that the strength of the social work profession will derive primarily from the power and effectiveness of its knowledge and skill base. Social work is currently characterized by a weak and diffuse knowledge base (Peterson, 1976; Rosen, 1969). Lewis (1972, pp. 71-72) observes, "Social work can be an exciting enterprise, reflecting the tensions and temptations associated with shaping the human service environment, capturing the mystery of the linkage between the heart and head in human action. . . . Although we anticipate an enthusiastic response from the users of our services and from our students and faculties as to the experience of social work practice and education, too often we hear criticism alerting us to the absence of these qualities. There is doubt that we know, or can claim to know, and doubt that we practice what we profess. These doubts gnaw at our insights and drain our convictions, depleting our intellectual and emotional enthusiasms."

I have focused my research on the profession's knowledge foundation component because I assume this component will prove most critical for the profession's future growth and development. A brief summary of my intent is made by Kahn (personal communication, December 1975): "I wanted you to know that I have read the research piece on the function of editorial boards, and I am delighted with it. Your findings confirm exactly what I have felt as I have watched the response of several editorial boards in social work and have noted the general decline of scholarship in a few of the journals. I hope, therefore, that you will publish rather rapidly, so there may be serious discussion of the implications of what you have found." Yet these findings met considerable resistance to attempts to publish them in social work journals (see Lindsey, 1977b). Eventually, these were published in journals outside my own field of social work. It is unfortunate that a controversy so vital to the social work profession had to be conducted outside of its main professional journals (see Lindsey, 1977b).

Conclusion

I constructed a measure of participation and influence in the manuscript review process (termed *editorial power*). Regression analysis with editorial power as the dependent variable indicated a different approach to editorial board appointments in psychology, social work, and sociology. Psychology journals appear to appoint individuals characterized by superior records of scientific achievement more to enhance the prestige of the journals than to attain assistance in the manuscript review process. On sociology journals, all board members appear to participate and influence the editorial decision making. Finally, social work journals appear to appoint individuals because of the powerful administrative positions they hold. In addition, there is a substantial qualitative bias among those board members appointed in social work.

The data presented in this chapter provide evidence that scientific achievement is a prerequisite for participation in the publication review process, at least in sociology and psychology. However, scientific achievement is not particularly helpful in accounting for the distribution of power among those who do participate in the review proceedings even in these two fields. For an understanding of the factors that account for the variations in editorial power among referees, the search will have to shift away from the direction suggested by normative theory. Four areas that have not been sufficiently considered within the traditional models of science but that could prove productive include

1. The impact of ideology and political values both internal and external to the editorial board (Blume, 1974; Bernal, 1939)
2. The potential bias of methodological orientations (see Chapter Three)
3. The boundary maintenance function served by referees with regard to the paradigms of the field (Kuhn, 1962; Law, 1974; Lodahl and Gordon, 1972)
4. The influence of the industriousness and promptness of the referee (Rodman, 1970)

These issues will be examined in Chapter Seven.

6

Products of
the Scientific
Publication System

*For those who are working at the research front, publi-
cation is not just an indicator but, in a very strong sense,
the end product of their creative effort. Whatever a
scientist may discover—however great or small his contribution—becomes effective only through being published, judged, incorporated somehow into the stock of
knowledge and used by his peers.*
—Price, 1974, p. 410

Editors select from among the large number of submitted manuscripts those few to be set in print and distributed to the scientific community. Through this gatekeeping process, journal
editorial boards confer authority and legitimacy on ideas. What
are those manuscripts like that are able to pass through the
highly selective screening process in the social and behavioral
sciences? To examine this question, articles were analyzed from
the fields of biochemistry, economics, psychiatry, psychology,
social work, and sociology. Inclusion of these additional fields
should serve to broaden the discussion, as well as provide a

The research reported in this chapter was done in collaboration with
Herbert Staulcup, John Morris, and William Short.

backdrop against which to compare the articles within the social and behavioral sciences.

Previous social studies of science have focused on the social stratification system that governs mobility within the scientific community (Hargens and Hagstrom, 1967; Cole and Cole, 1973), on the development of specialities (Edge and Mulkay, 1976), the emergence of new fields (Mullins, 1973), the complex network of relations that characterize specialty groups (Narin, Pinski, and Gee, 1976; Hargens, Mullins, and Hecht, 1978), and other social aspects of the scientific community. These efforts have led to the creation of the subfield of the sociology of science and related offshoots such as the psychology of science (Maslow, 1966; Mahoney, 1976), policy studies of science (Spiegel-Rosing and Price, 1977), and so on. In this chapter, I shall take a different perspective from those used in these studies—a microscopic perspective. Rather than examine the interactions of scientists, I will look at the products of these interactions—the scientific articles.

It has been assumed in the social studies of science that an article is an article—that empirical studies need only to count them. Yet, as will be seen in this chapter, the variation among articles is quite substantial. Research strategies that simply count articles and thus implicitly treat them all as roughly equal are bound to be plagued by imprecision and error, especially when comparing across disciplines. This partly explains the substantial coefficients of alienation in the models discussed in Chapter Five and similar findings in empirical studies in the sociology of science. In addition, citations to articles take on a different meaning across fields.

The Characteristics of Journal Articles

In order to examine the characteristics of journal articles, a cohort of periodical literature was selected. A cohort model was used in order to include citation information on the articles; the cohort sample provides a common base for comparison of the citation data (Glenn, 1977). Since the *Social Science Citation*

Index (Institute for Scientific Information, 1969–1976) has been back-dated to 1970, the sampling procedure selected a representative group of published articles that appeared in the professional literature during the calendar year 1970. Within each sample stratum of journals, sampling was performed without replacement.

The journals covered in the SSCI for 1970 comprised the sample frame for the social and behavioral sciences. The *Science Citation Index* (Institute for Scientific Information, 1970–1976) was used for the field of biochemistry. All professional journals in the English language were included in the sample stratum in each field. Sample strata were initially identified by their listing in the SSCI or SCI. Journals listed in the SSCI or SCI for each stratum were then compared with respective journal entries in *Ulrich's International Periodical Directory* (1973). The resulting cross entries embody the sample frame for each stratum.

With the journals selected, a proportional, stratified, random sample of between 130 and 200 articles was drawn from each field. (The target size of each subsample was 150. However, with only rough estimates of the total number of articles in each field, and using a proportionate draw, it was not possible to be precise on subsample size.) Since the number of journals in social work was small, all articles in this field were included. Each journal identified through the cross-listing procedure was drawn from. The proportionate size of the draw from each journal was estimated from a count of the number of journals in each field. No more than ten articles were selected from any one journal.

Measurements.   The approach of this exploratory study has been to collect as complete a set of information as reasonably possible on the cohort of literature. This included information on the number of words in an article (estimated by counting the words on one page and multiplying by the number of pages), the number of authors, the number of tables and graphs, the source by field of literature cited, whether the article acknowledged outside funding support, self-citations, the number of citations attracted between 1970 and 1976 (both within and outside the particular field of the article), information about the

authors similar to that collected on editors in Chapters Four and
Five, and the publication dates of the articles listed in a cohort
article's references. Data on articles were aggregated by journals;
information on the journals was also collected: the number of
papers published per year, average number of words per article,
subscription cost, number of words published per year (using
the estimate procedure applied to articles), and whether the
journal charged page fees. When available, ratings of the journals were collected. These data, coupled with the data collected
on the articles, allow for a detailed spectroscopic examination
of the scientific paper.

Findings

One of the first characteristics examined was the length of
articles. Table 13 shows that the typical article in biochemistry
is substantially shorter than the typical article in sociology but
not that different from the typical article in psychology. Articles
in sociology and economics run about 30 to 40 percent longer
than articles in other fields.

TABLE 13.   Length of Articles by Field

| | Number of Words | | | |
Field	Median	Mean	SD ^{a}	N ^{b}
Biochemistry	2,710	3,191	1,793	155
Economics	4,901	4,916	2,073	154
Psychiatry	3,331	3,858	2,308	182
Psychology	2,901	3,260	2,080	205
Social Work	3,600	3,871	1,631	346
Sociology	4,949	5,179	2,311	137

^{a}SD represents standard deviation.
^{b}N equals the number of articles in the subsample of the cohort.

Table 14 shows that there is much more outside funding
for research in biochemistry than in the fields of social inquiry.
Almost three quarters of the published papers acknowledged

TABLE 14. Characteristics of Articles in Different Fields

Field	Acknowledge Outside Funding	Quantitative Analysis [a]	Includes Table	Includes Graph
Biochemistry	74.2%	98.1%	73.5%	91.0%
Economics	34.3	72.1	46.8	39.6
Psychiatry	17.0	30.2	39.7	17.0
Psychology	43.4	75.1	70.7	41.5
Social Work	13.0	14.2	22.8	5.2
Sociology	27.0	52.6	65.0	22.6

[a]Article contained a statistical or mathematical analysis other than a percentage.

such support. It would normally be expected that the acknowledgement of funding in biochemistry would be reduced because of the policy of many of the journals to charge page fees *conditioned* on grant funding. Further, approximately 25 percent of the biochemistry articles were produced by non American authors, and more than one third of the non-American authors were from socialist or communist countries, where the acknowledgement of outside funding is not typical.

The applied fields of social inquiry (psychiatry and social work) acknowledged the lowest percentage of outside funding, in contradiction to the common wisdom that these subject areas attract substantial grant funding for research (Oromaner, 1974b). Among the social and behavioral science disciplines, psychology is apparently the most successful in obtaining outside funding for research, followed by economics and sociology respectively.

The most distinguishing characteristic of the literature in biochemistry is the use of quantitative analytic procedures. Reading the literature in this field, one is repeatedly introduced to differential equations and formulas that illustrate or analyze biochemical processes. In contrast, the applied fields of social inquiry are characterized by a relative absence of quantitative analysis. Although the increased use of quantitative analysis has been advocated by influential leaders in the social and behavioral sciences (Lastrucci, 1970), the presence of quantitative analysis should not be equated with science (Kuhn, 1961). Ravetz (1971, p. 158) observes that these advocates "have sincerely believed that real science is done by putting masses of quantitative data through a statistical sausage machine, and then observing the laws which emerge. From such caricatures of the process of scientific inquiry are derived criteria of adequacy that enforce an apparently rigorous procedure of research but whose results rarely escape vacuity. Such programs of reduction and mathematization base their claims on the undoubted successes of the physical sciences since the seventeenth century; but they ignore the long series of dismal failures in applying this approach to the sciences of life, thought, and society."

Among journal editors in social work, I found a powerful resistance to quantitative analysis (see Chapters Three and Five). It is not surprising, then, to find the quantitative approach missing from the literature in social work, as well as psychiatry; this may reflect the analytic needs of researchers and scholars in the applied fields (Lissitz, 1969). Or, as trustees of the standards of the scientific craft in their respective fields, these editors may be enforcing their methodological biases.

Among the social science disciplines, psychology and economics most use quantitative analytic procedures. The presence of tables and graphs in an article is a factor related to the use of quantitative analysis, and most of the biochemistry articles contained graphs, illustrations, or even color plates, all of which are very costly to prepare for publication. Nevertheless, it is clear that the use of quantitative procedures is not equivalent to the presence of tables and graphs. For example, in both sociology and psychiatry not all tables were used for the presentation of quantitative analytic material.

One of the major changes in the scientific literature during the last several decades has been the increase of multiple authorship (Price, 1963; Patel, 1972). Evidence of this is seen in Table 15. In biochemistry, more than 80 percent of the published papers had more than one author (for comparable findings, see Rudd, 1977). This reflects the fact that research in biochemistry is characterized by work teams operating in elaborate laboratories that require complex equipment, extensive funding, and a division of labor. In contrast, research in economics, social work, and sociology is mostly done by individuals operating alone and,

TABLE 15. Citations by the Number of Authors for Each Field.

Field	One Author		Two Authors		Three Authors		Four or More	
	Percent	Median	Percent	Median	Percent	Median	Percent	Median
Biochemistry	19	4.0	46	8.0	22	12.5	13	4.5
Economics	83	1.2	16	3.3	1	0.5	0	0.0
Psychiatry	53	1.0	27	0.7	9	4.0	10	3.2
Psychology	45	2.0	36	2.4	15	3.0	4	5.5
Social Work	75	0.5	20	1.0	4	1.3	2	1.5
Sociology	75	1.4	21	4.0	3	1.0	1	20.0

NOTE: $N = 1,179$. Median citation counts for the 1970 through 1975 period inclusive. The source for biochemistry data was the *Science Citation Index* (Institute for Scientific Information, 1970–1975).

for the most part, without expensive research apparatus. With respect to the social and behavioral sciences, psychiatry and psychology have almost half of their literature written by research teams, while in social work and sociology only one fourth of the literature is written by more than one author.

I have included in Table 15 data on the average number of citations to articles at various levels of multiple authorship to indicate that there is no apparent relationship between the number of authors and the attraction of citations across fields (see Oromaner, 1974a), except in the applied fields of social work and psychiatry, where there does seem to be a consistent proportional increase in citations attracted and number of authors. In biochemistry, where almost everyone does multiple-author work, the 'influence of collaboration is to increase the number of citations attracted until more than three authors are involved, when citations appear to plateau and descend. Since the cohort subsamples are relatively small, there is no doubt a large random component in these data, and consequently these findings should be treated as suggestive and exploratory.

Another characteristic examined was the number of references. Table 16 shows that biochemistry has the highest average number of references per article. This is somewhat surprising, since the biochemistry articles were typically the shortest. Thus, biochemistry shows a much higher number of references per thousand words than the social and behavioral sciences. Economics articles have a surprisingly low number of references per article. In this respect, the literature in economics is similar

TABLE 16.   Total References Per Article by Field.

Field	Median	Mean	SD	Percent None
Biochemistry	21.0	23.7	13.1	0.0
Economics	13.8	15.3	12.4	3.9
Psychiatry	20.2	18.2	12.3	9.3
Psychology	18.5	15.0	10.1	2.0
Social Work	11.3	9.8	6.6	18.8
Sociology	15.4	22.1	19.8	2.9

to the literature in social work in that it does not refer extensively to previous work. A notable feature of the social work literature is the large number of articles that make no reference to previous work. The significance of the number of references per article or per thousand words is debatable. It may be that some fields have a "footnote fetish" that only clutters up the literature (Wiener, 1977). Others have argued that references reflect the foundation on which reported research is built; that is, they reflect cumulative knowledge development (Price, 1965; Tukey, 1962). Price (1967, pp. 202-203) writes, "While they are at the research front papers behave, as we know from citation network analysis, as if they were pieces in a jigsaw puzzle. Each paper fits on two or three closely knit previous papers, and in turn it becomes the point of departure for new research, so that old knowledge breeds new at a constant and rapid rate, which of course results in exponential growth of the literature. This is peculiarly true only for science—for subjects that are not so scientific, each piece of new knowledge is laid down on the basis of previous contributions that are by no means so recent nor so well linked together, so that breeding capability is diluted and weaker as well as being less tightly knit."

The articles in the different fields reflect, in large measure, the characteristics of their respective fields as a whole. Table 17 shows that biochemistry had the largest number of postdoctoral fellows and the lowest faculty-to-student ratio in graduate programs. This is partly because of the high level of external funding

TABLE 17.   Number and Position of American Scientists
in Four Fields in 1970.

Field	Number of Graduate Students	Number of Postdoctorates	Number of Doctoral Departments	Number of Graduate Faculty
Biochemistry	3,401	947	124	1,498
Economics	7,086	54	108	2,165
Psychology	12,656	272	152	3,330
Sociology	5,889	50	97	1,668

Source: National Science Foundation, 1971.

available to investigators in this field. Biochemists have been responsible for much of the medical research in such areas as cancer, heart disease, and other crippling or fatal diseases. Their success in these applied areas has earned them considerable public support for continued research.

In contrast, support for education and research in the social and behavioral sciences is much less. Although one-fourth of the scientists in the United States are engaged in these fields, they receive less than one-third as much support per scientist as those in other fields (National Academy of Sciences, 1976, p. 14). Postdoctoral education and training, which is common in biochemistry, is the exception in the social and behavioral sciences. The faculty-to-student ratio is much higher in the social and behavioral sciences and highest in sociology. In large measure, the figures in Table 17 reflect government and private support for research and study in these fields. Evidently research resources have been more available in the hard and apolitical sciences.

In the preceding discussion, I have examined the different scientific fields as they are structured in the United States. The reason for this restriction is only because comparable data from other countries are not available. In the following section, I would like to examine the characteristics of the journals in these fields and relate it to the preceding discussion. Therefore, I will restrict the discussion to journals whose primary audience is American or that are published in the United States. The sample for this discussion is the same one used for the literature cohort, except that at this juncture I am examining the journals as a whole, not selected articles within them. The characteristics of the journals reflect their respective fields and add to our understanding of the distinctiveness of the various fields (see Hagstrom, 1970; Hargens, 1975).

The data in Table 18 indicate a great difference in the volume of literature produced in various fields. The estimated number of words published in biochemistry far exceeds that published in the fields of social inquiry.* This is puzzling, since

*The estimated number of words was determined by multiplying the average number of words per page for a particular journal by the number of pages published in calendar year 1970 by that journal and summing across journals.

TABLE 18. Characteristics of U.S. Journal Literature by Field.

Field	Number of Journals	Estimated Number of Words Per Year	Mean Library Subscription Rate	Mean Rejection Rate [a]	Estimated Number of Articles Per Year
Biochemistry	17	36,299,815	$71.70	29%[b]	11,376
Economics	20	6,351,100	15.50	69	1,292
Psychiatry	25	7,240,025	14.93	–[c]	1,877
Psychology	32	13,501,700	18.40	70	4,142
Social Work	9	1,703,070	7.50	80[d]	440
Sociology	17	5,733,325	11.00	78	1,107

[a] The source for these data is Zuckerman and Merton (1971, p. 76).
[b] The figure here is for bioscience, rather than biochemistry.
[c] Not available.
[d] This figure is derived from questionnaire information from editors discussed in Chapter Four.

there are fewer graduate students or faculty in biochemistry. It indicates that a much smaller-group in biochemistry is producing a literature several times larger than that in any of the social and behavioral fields. This is partly explained by the much lower rejection rate in biochemistry. (The data here are from Zuckerman and Merton, 1971, who do not provide a breakdown within the biosciences.) Since 70 percent of the papers submitted to journals in this field are published, a greater portion of what is written in this field is eventually set in print, most of it in the major journals. The high rejection rates in the social and behavioral sciences indicate the opposite in those fields. Further, the rejection rates of 80 percent do not take into account the sponsored submissions, inside-track submissions, and back-region communication discussed by Rodman and Mancini (1977), which allow a substantial part of the 20 percent of accepted manuscripts to have an edge on the normal submissions. Taking these "advantaged" submissions into account may increase the rejection rates by as much as 10 percent.

How can biochemistry support such a volume of literature? Part of the explanation is found in how the biochemistry journals are financed. As was shown earlier, there is a much greater level of outside support acknowledged in the biochemistry literature. Moreover, the policy of assigning page fees conditioned on these funds provides the biochemistry journals with substantial additional support. In fact, the National Science Foundation is sufficiently concerned with the amount of funds that go into publication to be investigating ways to reduce this expenditure (National Science Foundation, 1975; McCartney, 1976). The biochemistry journals also charge a much higher institutional subscription rate, on the average, than do the journals in the other fields (see Clasquin and Cohen, 1977, for similar findings in physics and chemistry). This may be partly justified by the fact that the biochemistry journals are, in terms of the number of words published per year, more lengthy. (For example, one of the major biochemical journals, not included in Table 18 because it is published in The Netherlands, contained an estimated 10,228,750 words—more than all the words published in any of the other fields except psychology.)

The data in Table 18 indicate differing opportunities for investigators in different fields to publish their results. For example, if we initially define the number of working scientists in a field as roughly equal to twice the number of faculty in graduate departments, then the number of articles published per year divided by the number of working scientists would provide a very rough estimate of the number of article spaces per working scientist. In biochemistry, that number for 1970 would be 3.8, whereas in the other fields of social inquiry it would be less than 0.5, except for psychology where it would be 0.6. If we look at the number of authorship spaces per year, this figure increases two- or threefold in biochemistry, because of multiple authorship. There are more available spaces in the literature for the biochemist than the social or behavioral scientist.

These figures must be viewed with some caution—they are very rough estimates. In biochemistry, there are a large number of nonacademic working scientists in medical research laboratories, pharmaceutical companies, and so on. Probably as much as 50 percent of biochemists are in such positions (which is why the number of graduate faculty was doubled to estimate the number of working scientists). Similar estimation problems occur in the social and behavioral sciences. There are a large number of undergraduate faculty in these fields, who write articles that compete for the available article space (thus, here too the estimate of working scientists from graduate faculty was doubled, which is undoubtedly conservative).

The social and behavioral science journals would do well to learn from the biochemistry journals regarding financing. The announced policy of the *Journal of Biological Chemistry*, found on the inside front cover, is typical: "All authors whose research is supported, fully or in part, by funds which can be used to pay page charges are expected to honor such billings at the rate of $35 per page. The billing for page charges is completely independent of the editorial offices of the journal. None of the editors have any contact with page charge billing and their collection, and no editor knows whether any author has paid the charge. Payment of page charges is not in any way a condition for publication." Only a few of the social and behavioral science journals charge page fees conditioned on grant funding, thus losing a large potential source of income.

In addition, the social and behavioral science journals might begin to charge increased institutional rates for subscriptions. The subscription rates charged by major journals to institutions would not greatly influence subscription levels, for most of the subscribing institutions would be reluctant to discontinue their subscriptions to journals central to particular fields (Clasquin and Cohen, 1977; Berg, 1970). If these journals substantially increased their institutional subscription rates, they would have resources to open up increased publication opportunities for scientists in their fields (where there are manuscripts that are seeking, but not finding, publication outlets because of high rejection rates forced, in part, by limited page allocations). This recommended change in subscription costs would not be as useful for new publications, since these are optional, rather than required, in most library collections.

The argument here is that the social and behavioral sciences would benefit from the expansion of publication opportunities—that there are research contributions that merit publication but are not published because of restricted publication outlets. However, a number of observers disagree with this (Cole and Cole, 1972). Hargens (1975) has examined the publication practices in three fields (chemistry, mathematics, and political sicence) and concluded the high rejection rates in the social sciences reflect a lack of normative integration in these fields. He writes (1975, p. 20), "When scientists agree on the identity and importance of various research questions in their field, and also on the strategies and techniques to investigate them, they will be able to produce research which is received as a contribution to knowledge. But, when they do not agree on these standards, judgments that particular papers do not constitute contributions to knowledge will be more frequent, and the rejection rates of their journals will be higher."

Price (1961) has argued that a saturation point for growth has been reached in the physical and biosciences. In this condition of saturation, Price (1963, p. 121) has argued against the need for additional support for growth in science: "Even if there were declared a sudden moratorium on pure scientific research, there would still be enough of a corpus of knowledge to provide for technical applications for several generations to come." Moreover, he argues that what additions could be made would be limited by a powerful law of diminishing returns. That law proposes that the proportion of published scientific articles that are "good" increases only as the square root of the total number of published articles. That is, the rate of increase equals (square root of N)/(N); thus, as N tends to infinity, the ratio tends to zero. (Gilbert and Woolgar, 1974, provide a useful review and assessment of the models of scientific growth advanced by Price, 1963, and others.)

Nonetheless, I am arguing for additional publication outlets for research currently done in the social and behavioral sciences that is frozen out because of space limitations. Journals serve both for the dissemination of knowledge and to certify the merit of research published. In this respect, the shortage of journal space in the social and behavioral sciences limits the ability of investigators in these fields to disseminate their findings and to receive the credit that is accorded such dissemination (Hamelman and Mazze, 1972).

The field of social work is characterized by the smallest volume of published literature. However, there are indications that the picture in this field is changing rapidly. Else (1978) has examined the state of journal publication in social work and found a sizable increase in the number of journals published. According to Else, eighteen of the twenty-nine journals published in social work (as of 1978) were initiated within the last five years. These new journals create an opportunity for social work to bridge the gap between concern with practice methodologies and the application of social science knowledge on the one hand and the careful and creative effort of empirical research on the other. The availability of additional publication outlets will attract increasing numbers of social work scholars and researchers and social scientists to issues of concern to the social work profession (Khinduka, 1977).

Citations to Articles

Citations for the literature cohort were collected for the period 1970 to 1976. The data are summarized in Table 19. The most salient finding is the difference between the mean and median citation counts in all fields. Citations to articles are highly skewed, as has been aptly demonstrated by Price (1963) and others. As might be expected from the previous discussion, the average paper in biochemistry attracts more citations than the typical paper in the social and behavioral sciences; the field with the lowest overall median citation count is social work. However, citation counts are of limited value in comparative studies (see Methodological Note at end of book). For example, the primary reason for the low citation count for social work articles has to do with the common practice by social work authors of making limited use of social work papers in constructing their articles. In a critical note on an earlier report of some of the comparative data on the accomplishments of editors in different fields found in Chapter Four, Gilbert (1977, p. 1109) observed, "The study is rather like matching sprinters and boxers in a 100-yard dash . . . calculating the results, and concluding that sprinters are better athletes." His point is that publication and citation counts are useful for comparison within fields but have limited utility for cross-discipline comparisons.

The data in Table 19 also indicate a variation in the use of studies in one field by other fields. In this regard, biochemistry is a remarkably interdisciplinary field, which is not surprising, as it arose through the merging of biology and chemistry (Fruton, 1976). The applied social sciences, social work and psychiatry, seem to be less cited by journals outside their field than the academic disciplines (Fliedner, 1976; Hamelman and Mazze, 1973).

Although the typical article in biochemistry attracts more citations than the typical article in the social and behavioral sciences, the shape of the distribution of citations within fields is similar. In all of the fields, 10 percent of the papers attracted 42 to 49 percent of the citations. Most of the papers that are published are rarely, if ever, used by future investigators (see Figure 4 in Measurement Note).

TABLE 19. Total Citations to Cohort Articles by Field.

Field	Citations Within Field			Citations Outside Field			Total Citations	
	Mean	Median	Total	Mean	Median	Total	Mean	Median
Biochemistry	9.2	3.4	1,426	9.3	3.9	1,446	18.5	8.7
Economics	4.4	1.3	670	1.3	0.2	193	5.6	1.6
Psychiatry	3.9	1.4	702	0.7	0.1	120	4.5	1.5
Psychology	7.9	2.8	1,620	1.2	0.3	252	9.1	3.2
Social Work	1.1	0.5	382	0.5	0.1	164	1.6	0.8
Sociology	4.0	1.7	542	2.4	0.5	333	6.4	2.3

Why does the typical article in biochemistry attract more citations than the typical paper in the social and behavioral sciences? There are several reasons for the difference. For one thing, as has been shown, there are many more articles in biochemistry published per year, and they contain, on the average, more references. Also, there are more citations to biochemistry articles from nonbiochemistry journals—there is greater interdisciplinary contact (Narin, Pinski, and Gee, 1976). These factors contribute to a greater pool of potential citers (Dieks and Chang, 1976) and thus to more citations. An additional reason has to do with the half-life of the literature in these fields (Burton and Kebler, 1960). The literature cited in biochemistry is much more recent (MacRae, 1969; Price, 1970). Thus, within a seven-year period the biochemistry article will attract more of its lifetime citations than will articles in other fields. The half-life characteristic is a reflection of the scientific effort in these different fields. In biochemistry, there is a rapidly moving research front; investigators are quickly responding to the contributions of others to push forward research in a particular area. In contrast, in the social and behavioral sciences, there is a substantial lag between the completion of research and its being reported in the literature. There is a heavier reliance on older, more theoretical analysis and thus a greater concern with producing enduring scholarship.

In an attempt to identify the factors that influence the number of citations an article attracts, I explored several different variables from the cohort of literature. I consistently found that information on the characteristics of the authors of an article seemed to have little value in predicting citations (in no case was it significant). It should be noted that this analysis was complicated by the phenomena of multiple authorship. How are the various author characteristics to be treated? Although I do not examine this issue here, it is a problem that is fundamental to empirical studies in the sociology of science (Beaver and Rosen, 1978).

The most useful variables in this exploratory analysis were the structural characteristics of the article. To illustrate, in the field of psychology almost 25 percent of the variation ($R^2 = .24$)

TABLE 20. Determinants of the Number of Citations
Attracted by Psychology Articles.

Article Characteristic	Beta Weight	Simple Correlation
Number of words	.364 $p < .01$	.445
Graphs present	.253 $p < .01$	.332
Total references	.118 $p < .05$	.245
Use of case example	−.143 $p < .05$	−.134

NOTE: Number of citations were log transformed; $R^2 = .295$; $N = 205$.

in the number of citations an article was able to attract could be predicted from the number of words it contained. Table 20 contains the results of the regression analysis of citations with the variables that were significant from the exploratory analysis. In psychology, nearly one third of the variation in the number of citations an article was able to attract could be predicted from these structural characteristics. These data reinforce the findings reported in the Methodological Note (at the end of the book) that citations are quite problematic as a measure of "quality." Before citations are used as a measure of quality, more research is needed on exactly what citations measure.

The significant predictive variables for citations changed dramatically from discipline to discipline. For example, in psychiatry the number of authors on a paper was one of the best predictors, whereas for the other fields it was not predictive. Dovetailing with the previous findings, the presence of quantitative analysis was a significant predictor in social work (where the average number of citations for a paper with quantitative analysis was 2.35 [$N = 49$] and without it was 1.15 [$N = 297$]; in the other fields, it was not a useful predictor.

Conclusion

The data examined in this chapter vividly portray the wide variation among professional journals in different fields. In biochemistry, research is conducted by teams of investigators in expensive research laboratories with complex equipment and requires the rapid pursuit of new specialties and the expeditious writing up of the results. The research teams have a major concern with priority in publishing their new findings, and thus journals decide and publish rapidly. There is a tremendous amount of publishing among biochemists. The number of article spaces available per working scientist is far greater than in the social and behavioral sciences. Biochemists make use of a fast-changing and relatively new source of references, as seen in the short half-life of the published literature and the proportion of references less than five years old. There is more funding available for publication in biochemistry; the journals charge page fees conditioned on grant funding and have higher institutional subscription rates.

The social and behavioral science journals have been changing and now look more like the hard sciences. There has been an increase in the use of quantitative analysis, amount of multiple authorship, and the number of references per article (Patel, 1972; Price, 1963). However, these fields are not characterized by the type of fast-moving research front that requires team effort and specialization among collaborators. The articles in the social and behavioral sciences are longer, make less use of quantitative analysis, are built on an older literature, and have had less outside funding for their preparation.

The competition for publication in the social and behavioral sciences is much more intense than in biochemistry. The journals in these fields of social inquiry publish fewer articles and have higher rejection rates. Thus not all publishable research is published. The social and behavioral science journals might be able to facilitate both research and publishing in their fields by restructuring along the lines of the journals in biochemistry. In this regard, it would be useful for a couple of journals in the social and behavioral sciences to charge page fees conditioned on grant funding on an experimental basis and for the major journals to increase their institutional subscription rates and to use the additional revenue to open up increased publication outlets.

7

Reflections on Publication Review Proceedings and Recommendations for Reform

When considering the establishment of rules concerning blind review, conflict of interest, nepotism, and the like, it would . . . seem advisable to consider more than the possibility that some individuals in the system may be venal and corrupt. The protestations of even the most virtuous and disinterested participants that they are capable of independent judgments should be considered suspect.
—Nisbett and Wilson, 1977, p. 256

The decision making of professional journals is protected from public scrutiny by a confidential and anonymous review, and each board proceeds, in theory, like a jury with the fair and impartial review of manuscripts (see Levine, 1974). How well does the current peer review structure of review proceedings in the social and behavioral sciences actually protect against the intrusion of particularistic standards and theoretical or methodological bias? There is a long history of belief in the scientific community that the peer review system that governs the publication process provides a relatively fair and impartial assessment of submitted work (Mitroff and Chubin, 1978).

It is not uncommon to hear complaints of bias and incompetence from those who have had their manuscript rejected. As Schaeffer (1970, p. 362), writes, "Given two or three drinks, almost any researcher who does not publish regularly in APA journals can produce shocking tales of the unjust treatment accorded his, or his friend's, publication efforts." He adds, "APA defenders, of course, realize that these are just the sour grapes of a second-rate researcher." Do journal editors and referees express personal biases and prejudices in their review proceedings? Mahoney (1976) has argued that scientists, like other members of their species, may be characterized by confirmatory bias; that is, the tendency to be attentive to and supportive of what confirms one's view and to ignore or discredit what contradicts one's view.

In the publication review process, scientist–referees are able to exercise a great deal of authority. They determine what will go into the public record of science and be disseminated to others. In the exercise of this authority, the problem of confirmatory bias becomes particularly acute. As Kuhn (1962), Fisher (1966, 1967), and others have argued, there is a major element of compassion and commitment to ideas among scientists, especially if the ideas are the offspring of the scientists. The eminent scientists who serve as gatekeepers of the public forum of scientific exchange are not free of confirmatory bias. In fact, confirmatory bias may result in scientist–referees restricting admission to the public forum only to those who are sympathetic to the dominant paradigm, theoretical perspective, or currently accepted line of inquiry. Critics of the major approaches, or individuals developing new lines of analysis, may be thwarted by eminent scientists who have built their reputations on the traditional approaches (Barber, 1962; Mitroff, 1974). In the social sciences especially, where the acceptance rates are very low, one negative review can kill a manuscript's chance of acceptance, and the variety of theoretical perspectives increases the probability of conflicting points of view (Pfeffer, Leong, and Strehl, 1977; Hargens, 1975).

To examine if particularistic standards or bias intrude into the review process, we need a way to control the primary variables. As in most areas of applied research, it is quite difficult to manipulate a real situation for experimental purposes. Most of the previous research in this area has been sociological and dependent on survey and archival data (Crane, 1967; Abramowitz and Gomes, 1975). These data are quite limited in assessing the cardinal issue: To what extent do nonscientific criteria influence publication decisions? Mahoney (1977) set up an innovative experimental research design to examine the question of reviewer bias.

Mahoney's Pseudo-Paper Experiment

Working with the assistance of editors from the *Journal of Applied Behavioral Analysis* (JABA), Mahoney randomly assigned a sample of seventy-five reviewers to five experimental groups. The following list demonstrates Mahoney's design:

	Reported Results	Interpretation
Random Group 1	confirmatory	no discussion
Random Group 2	disconfirming	no discussion
Random Group 3	no results	no discussion
Random Group 4	mixed results	confirmatory
Random Group 5	mixed results	disconfirming

Five groups of referees read a manuscript that had been altered according to the experimental design. Introduction and methodology sections were identical for all pseudo-papers. The pseudo-paper was reviewed by an associate editor of JABA to ensure that the introduction and methodology sections were in accord with the standards of the journal.

Since the reviewers were drawn from JABA, a behavioral psychology journal, Mahoney selected a controversial topic from this field. At the time of the study, there was a debate in the behavioral psychology literature regarding the influence of behavioral reinforcers on intrinsic motivation. Some critics of behavioral techniques suggested that reinforcers had a detrimental effect on intrinsic motivation; when reinforcers were withdrawn, they claimed, the modified behavior diminished below natural levels. For example, children exposed to a new activity will express a natural desire to explore it if it has intrinsic interest. If the children are rewarded with externally administered reinforcers for engaging in the activity, then their intrinsic motivation will be diminished and replaced by the reinforcers. According to the critics, when the reinforcers are withdrawn, motivation to engage in the activity will cease, because it was contingent on the reinforcers.

According to the pseudo-paper that Mahoney sent to the reviewers in the experiment, children were exposed to two different activities, a play session with pressed blocks and a learning session with children's books, and were observed over a two-week period in order to establish a baseline. Then randomly selected groups were reinforced for engaging in the activities, while others were not. Later the reinforcers were withdrawn to determine if the level of activity of the reinforced children would decline below that of the nonreinforced children. In the confirmatory condition, the level of activity was found *not* to decline below baseline; whereas in the disconfirmatory group the activity was found to diminish below baseline. Data were said to be collected unobtrusively by closed-circuit camera and judged by independent raters. All versions of the pseudo-paper contained the same bibliography. All author-identifying information was removed. The pseudo-papers were exactly alike except on the experimentally manipulated dimensions. When the data reported in the pseudo paper supported the reviewer's prejudices, they were termed *confirmatory*; when the data conflicted with the reviewer's belief, they were called *disconfirmatory*.

What did Mahoney (1977) find? Sixty-seven evaluations were obtained from seventy-five reviewers. All five of the experimental groups rated several components of the pseudo-paper: (1) relevance of the topic, (2) methodology, (3) presentation of the data, (4) scientific contribution, and (5) overall recommendation for publication. All of the groups rated the relevance of the topic quite high. On the other components of the pseudo-paper, however, there were differences in ratings.

When evaluating the exact same methodology, reviewers rated confirmatory results consistently higher than disconfirmatory results. This finding, however, did not attain statistical significance. On the dimension of presentation of data, papers with data that reported confirmatory results were rated much higher than papers reporting disconfirmatory findings, and at a level of statistical significance. In other words, if the data reported in the pseudo-paper were in accord with the theoretical leanings of the reviewer, there was a higher likelihood of the data presentation being favorably rated. The interpretation of the data did not appear to influence this rating. Irrespective of the discussion of the results, confirmatory findings were rated high, while disconfirmatory findings were rated low.

Mahoney's experiment (1977) indicates that it is not so much how the investigator interprets the data that influences the rating of a paper but, rather, what the data indicate. If the findings contradict the reviewer's theoretical leanings, he or she will give a less favorable review, irrespective of how the findings are interpreted. This is a cause for concern, for it suggests that reviewers are not so much troubled by authors' exaggerated claims as by their actual findings, over which, ideally, the investigator exercises no control.

Item analysis of the five dimensions indicated a consensus among the reviewers' scores within the experimental groups, except on the dimension of final recommendation (Mahoney, 1977). This indicates that the final decision is not a summed value of the ratings of the various dimensions but derives from a gestalt closure that is not necessarily equal to the sum of the evaluations given on the separate parts. (This would suggest that the proposal for a checklist inventory that could be scored by a well-trained clerk—see Wolff, 1973; Bowen, Perloff, and Jacoby, 1972—may not be in conformity with the approach used by most reviewers.)

On this crucial dimension of *recommendation for publication*, Mahoney (1977, p. 161) writes, "Here again a familiar pattern emerged. Identical manuscripts suffered very different fates depending on the direction of their data. When they were positive [confirmatory], the usual recommendation was to accept with moderate revisions. Negative [disconfirmatory] results earned a significantly lower evaluation, with the average reviewer urging either rejection or major revision."

As a result of a typographical error in preparing the pseudo-paper, an unplanned variable was introduced: Triads were reported formed among subjects assigned to treatment groups, yet the groups were not divisible by three. Consequently, Mahoney was able to assess whether the detection of a technical error was contingent on the bias of the reviewer. Of those who read a confirmatory pseudo-paper, 25 percent detected the problem. Of those who read a disconfirmatory paper, 71 percent detected the problem. The difference is statistically significant.

On the completion of the experiment, Mahoney wrote to his subjects informing them of the true nature of the requested review. In his letter, he asked the subjects: (1) for their reviews of the study, (2) their assessment of the reliability of their evaluation in comparison with other reviewers, and (3) whether they would like to see a final report of the study. Of the subjects, 85 percent replied to this inquiry. Of the fifty-seven respondents, thirteen expressed a negative reaction (primarily because of the deception), and four stated they were suspicious. This concern is particularly puzzling among behavioral psychologists, who routinely use similar experimental strategies in their own work. The majority of the subjects responded favorably, and all requested a copy of the final results. In a later report, Mahoney (1978, p. 41) wrote, "A handful were not so convivial. One sent back my letter with the word *bullshit* stamped all over it. Three others filed complaints with the APA ethics committee. Two wrote letters to my department chairperson. And one made phone calls to the dean and president of the university, demanding that I be fired."

When asked to predict their interreferee agreement with others on identical dimensions, the reviewers recorded estimates between .69 to .74. In this regard, their estimates of reliability are similar to those of Stinchcombe and Ofshe (1969) for the journal review process. Empirical studies of the review process in the social and behavioral sciences have consistently indicated a much lower interrater reliability—approximately .25 (see Chapter Four). For the reviewers in this experiment, the results ranged from -.07 to .30 on the several dimensions assessed.

In summarizing his experimental findings, Mahoney (1977, p. 174) concludes, "It was found that (1) referee evaluations may be dramatically influenced by such factors as experimental outcome and (2) interreferee agreement may be extremely low on factors relating to manuscript evaluation."

In Chapter Two, I argued that journals have historically served as a major source of critical scientific dialogue. When a scientist publishes results in a journal, readers may critically scrutinize the arguments. If there is a disagreement, the concerned scientist can replicate the study and report additional findings, write a letter to the editor pointing out the limitations of the study, or conduct a comparative study. In every case, the journal facilitates open exchange and criticism of ideas. This is an essential characteristic of a healthy scientific community.

Popper (1963) has demonstrated the importance of criticism to the health and vitality of science. In this regard, Popper has developed the notion of a *critical attitude*, which he defines as the willingness and commitment of a scientist to open up his or her own views to severe scrutiny. He proposed that this critical attitude is what differentiates the practitioners of science and of pseudo-science. Ravetz (1971, p. 277) has commented, "In the years since his [Popper's] first insight, the question of the personal motives of scientists has been seen as rather more complex and the demarcation correspondingly less neat. But we can agree with his basic insight and restate the dichotomy on a practical, rather than epistemological, basis. Then we can say that the absence of a critical attitude among the members of a scientific community is a *cause* of a degeneration into vacuity and corruption."

Mahoney's findings suggest that the forum for critical scientific dialogue may be undermined by the impassioned methodological and theoretical persuasions of editorial board members (see Mitroff, 1974). Kuhn (1962) has shown that it is not necessarily irrefutable evidence that leads toward paradigm shifts in science but rather the passing from the scientific community of the theorists who hold the traditional view. Mahoney's study lends additional support to Kuhn's view. The ideal of scientific knowledge developing in a context of fair and impartial review of competing theories and supporting evidence becomes problematic in light of empirical study of the actual operations of the science journals.

How shall we protect the journal publication system in the social and behavioral sciences from particularistic and biased standards of assessment? The health and vitality of science demands that scientists have faith and respect for the critical institutions making the decisions that shape their career and professional enterprise (Gustin, 1973). Thus it is essential that scientists take an interest in assuring the integrity of the scientific enterprise. The bias Mahoney found must be protected against. How can this be accomplished? The first step is to recognize that the problem exists. (This recognition runs counter to the thrust of existing studies in the sociology of science, especially in studies of the physical sciences—see Cole and Cole, 1973. Yet the physical and biosciences are quite distinct from the social and behavioral sciences, and much of the conflicting findings in the sociology of science can probably be traced to this distinction.)

The Case for and Against Multiple Submission

The review process takes quite a long time. One way around the problem of delay is the submission of a manuscript to several journals simultaneously. This runs counter to a strong tradition in the sciences against multiple submission. Professional associations such as the American Psychological Association (APA) and the American Sociological Association (ASA) have adopted policies expressly prohibiting multiple submission. However, it may prove instructive to examine the pros and cons of a policy of multiple submission.

The advantage of multiple submission is that it would

allow more authors a better chance of having their papers accepted. The more journals that review a given manuscript, the greater the probability of receiving an acceptance—and an author only needs *one* acceptance. In addition, if multiple submission were common practice, journals would be in competition for good papers. A free-market situation would exist, with major journals competing with minor journals for the best papers. As it is now, authors usually develop a hierarchy of journals that might accept a given paper and then work their way down the list (Kochen and Tagliacozzo, 1974). This approach gives the prestigious journals a decided competitive advantage. Peters (1976) has argued that a policy against multiple submission is a policy in constraint of free trade.

Editors of the American Sociological Association's journals, meeting in 1974, discussed the imprecision of the manuscript review process, the excessively long review periods, and the overload of manuscript submissions (Turner, 1976). At these meetings, it was argued that the current frustrating conditions would get out of hand if the traditional practice of single submission was increasingly violated. Apparently there was some evidence at the time that multiple submissions had occurred. In order to protect itself against this, the ASA Publications Committee asked the ASA Council to establish a policy against multiple submission. The council responded that such a policy would have to be balanced by a commitment on the part of editors to a reasonable review time (correspondence to the council from Rodman may have been important here).

Shortly after this agreement, the ASA Council adopted the following policy stated on the inside front cover of their journals: "*ASA Multiple-Submissions Policy:* Submission of a manuscript to a professional journal clearly implies commitment to publish in that journal. The competition for journal space requires a great deal of time and effort on the part of editorial readers whose main compensation for this service is the opportunity to read papers prior to publication and the gratification associated with discharge of professional obligation. For these reasons, the American Sociological Association regards submission of a manuscript to a professional journal while that paper is under review by another journal as unacceptable [underscore in original] ."

Since this policy only codified tradition, there has not been much discussion of it. Turk (1976) observes that a conspiracy was not involved in the adoption of this policy, but adds (p. 169) that "The ASA policy statement certainly cannot be taken seriously as a defense of the policy." There may be reasons to support the ASA multiple-submission policy, but those provided in the policy statement do not suffice. Rather, they reflect the interests of the review board members. Rodman (personal communication, April 1978) has pointed out that while the ASA journals regularly publish the ban against multiple submissions, the balancing commitment to speedy review is not published. If the decision on multiple submissions were to be made by the full membership of the ASA, one could well imagine a different policy and rationale.

Peters (1976) has written a careful and systematic criticism of the policy and in the process catalyzed a debate in the *American Sociologist*. Basically, he argues that the rationale used to support the policy has a number of fallacies. To begin with, he proposes that submission of a paper to a journal implies no commitment to publish in that journal. Rather, it asks the journal to review the manuscript to consider whether it would be willing to publish the paper. In this regard, Peters argues, submission of a paper is like the submission of a vitae for consideration for employment; the act expresses an interest in employment but certainly not commitment.

There are a number of professional journals that do not require solo submission (Rhodes, 1974). In addition, there has been a tradition in the book-publishing trade of permitting multiple submission (Orlov, 1973, 1976). In this light, it is hard to accept the view that submission implies commitment | to publish. It would be more accurate to say that editors and referees are inconvenienced by multiple submission. They want to be sure that if they accept a manuscript they will subsequently be able to publish it. Otherwise, an additional step is introduced into the review process that increases the editors' already heavy workload. Since editors have control over a highly desired forum, they can establish rules that serve their own best interests. Peters argues the policy against multiple submissions is just that—a self-serving policy for the convenience of editors.

Peters also points out that the primary motivation for editors to serve on review boards is not the "opportunity to read papers prior to publication." Rather, board members serve because of the prestige that accrues to such service. However, there is disagreement about the precise value of this prestige. Turk (1976, p. 170) writes, "Why not admit openly that editing and reviewing do earn status points, and do provide opportunities to affect the nature and direction of the sociological enterprise?" In contrast, Stinchcombe (1976, p. 171) writes, "One's motivation is determined by whatever is scarce in one's life, but most reviewers already have lots of trivial status points to put on vitae. I would rather have more hours on warm island beaches—or under some uninfected Dutch elm trees—or have more spaghetti with clam sauce, than more papers to referee." Although there is disagreement about the motive to review papers, all agree it is not the opportunity of prior review that is primary.

A policy allowing multiple submission might require more reviewers, but obtaining reviewers' services has not been a severe problem for editors. For example, Levinsohn (1976, p. 177) writes, "There are many more readers out there. . . . In my last year at the AJS [American Journal of Sociology], we recruited more than 600 referees for fewer than 600 manuscripts." In the physical sciences, the recruitment of large numbers of reviewers has been routine practice for the journals. As Rodman (1970, p. 352) notes, *"The Physical Review* and *Physical Review Letters* have a list of 2,500 researchers for use as referees. A computer is used to keep track of their performances, and those who are habitually too slow are eliminated. . . . *Science* maintains an active list of 6,000 scientists. . . . *Nature* has a panel of 2,000 reviewers."

Peters, too, identifies the policy against multiple submissions as a policy in restraint of free trade, enforcing a monopolistic practice that favors the established prestigious journals, including the ASA journals, and his final argument is precisely that a policy allowing multiple submissions would foster competition among the journals to attract manuscripts. Those journals offering or providing expeditious and careful review would be in a competitive position: "Prompt response by smaller, less well-known journals may allow them to steal a march on the giants .... It is precisely the lengthy, tedious process of reviewing, revising, and resubmitting associated with the major journals that multiple submission is employed to circumvent" (Peters, 1976, p. 167).

The problem of the lengthy review process is the major concern among the general membership of the social and behavioral science professional organizations (Brackbill and Korten, 1970). In 1970, Rodman reported on a path-breaking experiment he conducted at *Social Problems* to see if he could do something to alleviate the excessive review time. When writing nominees for the editorial board, Rodman asked them to sign a statement promising that they would review manuscripts within two weeks. Twenty-four out of thirty-two signed the form. Of those who declined, none cited the review period requirement as their reason. Rodman's results were encouraging: "Looking at the results for the 384 manuscripts evaluated by referees who were on the editorial board, we see that . . . 71 percent of the manuscripts were handled by the referees within the agreed-on period, and 85 percent were handled within one week more than the agreed-on period" (1970, p. 355).

Although Rodman's experiment demonstrates that journal editors can carry out their moral responsibility to provide expeditious reviews, there are few incentives for editors, especially of the prestigious journals, to do so. Examining the *AJS*, Schwartz (1975, p. 68) writes, "There is no assumption among its editors that the speed with which it processes papers affects its ability to attract high-quality and significant material. In this respect, the journal is less dependent on authors than authors are on the journal. Accordingly, improvements in operations are generally made as a matter of principle, if and when they are made at all, and not in response to extrinsic considerations, like competition with other journals—to which a second thought has never been given."

Partly as a result of the absence of competition with other

journals, the *AJS* has been able to attract an increasing number of manuscripts, despite an average manuscript review period of 5.7 months in 1972. Paradoxically, Schwartz observed that as the *AJS* attracted more manuscripts it increased the length of its review period, with no apparent decline in the number of manuscripts submitted. As the journal is able to be more selective, its reputation increases, making it more attractive to authors. This leads to very lengthy lag times between the completion of a research project and the appearance of its results in the literature. The average time between the acceptance of a paper and its publication by the *AJS* was 12 months. If the *AJS* is typical of social and behavioral science journals, as I suspect it is, then the average time between completion of a research project and its appearance in the literature—if its hypothetical *true quality* (see Chapter Four) places the research report in the top 1 percent of such studies—is two years. For studies in the top 10 to 15 percent of hypothetical *true quality*, the lag time would be three or more years. This is an extraordinary delay in the reporting of scientific research. In the physical sciences, where the review period is much shorter, the lag time is probably less than 6 months for the average published study (Goudsmit, 1968; Ringle, 1969). As Rodman (1970, p. 352) has noted, "Publication of an article in the *Physical Review* took approximately 5 months from the time of submission, while letters were published in 2 to 3 months. Even this was considered too slow, and the pressur to publish fast and to establish priority claims led to the founding of *Physical Review Letters*, a weekly journal that reduced time from submission to publication to less than four weeks."

However, one advantage of the lengthening of the review process, as Schwartz (1975) has observed, has been the provision of extensive reviewers' comments, for it does not seem fair to keep a manuscript six months and then, if a negative disposition is made, to send only a formal rejection letter. Schwartz argues that *AJS* provides an educational function by providing these reviewers' comments. Turner (1976, p. 169) observes, "The most notable change in journal policies during my professional career has been the adoption of the practice of supplying authors with extended and penetrating evaluations of their manuscripts. This professional critiquing is an invaluable service for authors."

Returning to the question of multiple submissions, one consequence of a policy allowing it would be to undercut the value of the educational function of reviewers' comments. In fact, if such a policy were adopted, it would probably be at the expense of this very important educational function. It should be noted that not all journals provide this service. For example, most social work journals do not. (The new *Journal of Social Service Research* provides reviewers' comments as one of its features; see Khinduka, 1977. I would like to see more of the journals in social work adopt this procedure.) Especially when reviewers' comments are not provided, it seems quite unfair to ask for solo submission.

The loss of reviewers' comments is a high price to pay for a policy of multiple submission. Nor is it clear that a policy of multiple submission would ease access to publication outlets or increase a given manuscript's chances. Without an increase in the amount of journal space, a multiple-submission policy would only intensify the competition for existing journal space, limiting it to those authors with prestigious credentials. This has apparently been the effect of an overabundant supply of book-length manuscripts on the book-publishing industry (see Orlov, 1976; Powell, in press). According to Powell, the typical publishing firm in the social sciences, receiving as many as a hundred manuscripts and proposals for every one that it will publish, uses a garbage-can model of decision making to cope with the situation. Everything gets mixed around, and a haphazard selection process occurs. The adoption of this model of decision making in the journal enterprise would be harmful to science. (In fact, concern with the quality of scholarly books and monographs produced under these conditions has resulted in a national enquiry into the "spreading chaos" in scholarly publishing; see Van Dyne, 1975.) If this model is adopted by journals, authors will not be guaranteed a careful and impartial reivew of their work. Rather they will be vying for the attention of editors to their work. In this competition, those with prestigious credentials will receive the closest attention. Rather than equalizing access, there is the danger that multiple submissions may have just the reverse consequence.

Perhaps the problems that multiple submission is designed to solve could be better solved with an approach less costly to the educational function of the review process. Rodman (1970, p. 354) suggests that "Without hampering editorial freedom, professional associations that sponsor journals could require editors' annual reports to indicate the amount of time that elapses between receiving manuscripts and reporting decisions to authors; they could establish guidelines to limit the size of the backlog; they could insist on one-year renewable tenure for all members of the editorial board, with the requirement that those who are unavailable or dilatory be rotated off; they could advise incoming editors of the importance of routine procedures to follow up delayed reviews. They could also define undue delays as a breach of professional ethics." A reasonable policy might be to permit authors to submit their manuscripts to a second journal if they have not heard from the first journal within six or eight weeks. The limitation of this policy is that it may penalize the second journal if the first (tardy) journal finally offers acceptance after two or three weeks and thus preempts the second (innocent) journal. In this situation, the author would be responsible for quickly notifying the innocent journal and perhaps paying a nominal withdrawal fee.

Submission Fees and Page Fees

Beginning in 1978, the American Sociological Association's Council implemented a policy requiring a submission fee for journal review, which is stated on the inside front cover of their journals: "A processing fee of $10 is required for each paper submitted; such fees will be waived for student members of ASA. This reflects a policy of the ASA Council and Committee on Publications affecting all ASA jouranls. It is a reluctant response to the rapidly accelerating costs of manuscript reviewing. A check or money order, made payable to the American Sociological Association, should accompany each submission.

The fee must be paid in order for the review process to begin."
This is an innovative policy. The rationale for the policy is not
entirely clear, except that it eases the financial burden on the
journals. As with the policy against multiple submission, I would
speculate that this policy might not have been adopted had it
been put before the general membership. It is, in a sense, a regres-
sive tax that places an increased burden on scholars and researchers with limited access to funds without being a significant
additional source of funds for the journals. The policy will
dampen the incentive of scholars who are at less prestigious
institutions, who have limited access to funds, and who are for
those reasons already at a disadvantage in the publication review
proceedings (because of review imprecision matched with
particularistic standards, as discussed in Chapter Four). No
doubt, the policy of a submission fee will not materially affect
those who voted and implemented the policy—those who are at
the elite institutions and make up the council.

If the ASA-sponsored journals are suffering from a shortage of funds, there is a better way to obtain additional funds.
The tradition in the physical sciences of page fees conditioned
on grant funding, if adopted in the social and behavioral sciences,
would increase journal revenue more than the submission fee
policy, as well as place the burden on those who could most
afford it, without taxing authors.

While the physical sciences are characterized by a high
percentage of research supported by grant funding, the social
and behavioral sciences have been relatively neglected by, for
example, the National Science Foundation, which in fiscal year
1975 allocated only 5 percent of its total research obligations to
the social and behavioral sciences. Holton (1978, pp. 62-63)
observes, "This is obviously a highly charged topic, one that
soon would raise the question whether the Congress was wise to
be persuaded some years ago not to fund a separate Social
Science Foundation." Nonetheless, if authors in the social and
behavioral sciences who did acknowledge grant funding paid page
fees out of their grants, it would result in greater financial assistance to the journals than would the submission fee policy.

Summary and Recommendations

We have seen that the review process is imprecise, that bias intrudes into it, and that the time required for review of a submitted paper is often quite long, and we have looked at several proposed solutions to these problems. Multiple submissions might reduce manuscript review time for the author. However, a policy of multiple submissions is not without cost, for it would probably eliminate reviewers' comments, an important educational function currently provided by journals in sociology and psychology. Nor is it certain that a multiple-submissions policy would, as advocates suggest, produce a more open review system. Moreover, reduction of manuscript review time can be accomplished by simply requiring editors to review papers within a specified period.

The problem still remains of the apparent intrusion of bias and particularistic standards into the manuscript review process. The remainder of this chapter examines several proposals to reduce the amount not only of bias but also of carelessness in the review process. We may reasonably expect that bias and carelessness are two major components of imprecision in the review process.

How to Control Bias. First, during the last decade the social and behavioral science journals have widely adopted a policy of blind review (American Psychological Association, 1972). The policy of blind review ensures, to the extent possible, that the reviewer will not know who the author of a manuscript is. Thus characteristics of the author, which should be functionally irrelevant to the review process (Cole and Cole, 1973), are not allowed to enter in. The journals that do not observe this policy are the exception. The importance of blind review has been pointed up by studies of attribution theory in psychology (Nisbett and Wilson, 1977; Ross, 1977) that indicate that subjects asked to make judgments of others are powerfully influenced by social factors that should be irrelevant to the judgment process. Moreover, when confronted with this evidence of bias, subjects become even more adamant in asserting the absence of bias (Ross, Lepper, and Hubbard, 1975). In the current practice, unfortunately, the editor in chief, who has the very important initial function of sending a manuscript to particular referees, is not blind to the submitter. There is no compelling reason why the editor in chief should know the identity of the submitter either at the beginning or close of the review process (when the decision to publish is derived from reviewers' recommendations). If the clerical staff who receives the mail were to blind the editor in chief to author identity, there would be an additional and very important protection against bias, at no apparent cost to the efficient operation of the review process.

Second, Glenn (1976, p. 185) suggests that all papers have at least three reviewers: "Although the primary purpose of adding a third referee would be to detect flaws, it should also contribute to fairness, since the probability that all three referees will make unfair negative recommendations (because of carelessness or bias) is less than the probability that two referees will." I concur with his recommendation.

The addition of a third reviewer might also increase the likelihood of conflicting recommendations and thus rejection. Yet journals will fill their allocated space. The issue is the effectiveness of the space allocation procedure (the gatekeeping function). With two reviewers, the probability of rough agreement is relatively high (about 70 percent, see Crandall, in press). But the agreement has more to do with the underlying distributions that are crossed than with the reliability of reviewers' recommendations. For example, if a five-point scale is used, and the judgments of reviewers are normally distributed with a mean of 3 and a standard deviation of 1, then close to 50 percent of the judgments of two reviewers would fall in the same or adjoining categories. As Crandall (in press, p. 4) has pointed out, "The major problem with the optimistic interpretation of reviewer agreement presented here [well over 70 percent] is that, given the distributions of the ratings, a high level of interrater agreement would also be expected by chance." (This concurs with the Stinchcombe and Ofshe (1969) model presented in Chapter Four.) Use of three reviewers would limit the tendency to capitalize on chance agreement and should lead to greater overall precision. (I should note that the proper measure of the precision of reviewers' judgments is the conventional reliability coefficient used in the studies reported in Chapter Four. The logic of the reliability coefficients allows us to predict the first reviewer's judgment from knowledge of the second reviewer's judgment. The reliability coefficient provides a precise index of reliability. It penalizes discrepant judgment according to the magnitude of disagreement. The agreement model treats all discrepant judgments in the same fashion.)

Third, there is evidence that referees may be biased in their reviews, especially of controversial papers. An author who submits a paper that challenges major research or examines a controversial subject would do well to forewarn the editorial office so that an effort can be made to obtain reviews from both sides of the controversy. The author might even suggest potential reviewers from which the editor may select one or two. (Hendrick, 1976, p. 208, has found that "very little bias is introduced into the reviewing system by allowing authors to nominate their own reviewers.") An illustration of this problem is given by Meile (1977, p. 52): "With two colleagues, I submitted a paper, containing results critical of the work of an expert, to two journals sequentially. The comment of one referee appeared to be decisive in the rejection of the manuscript. The referee admitted that he had reviewed the manuscript for both journals, and we later learned that he was the very author whose research our paper had put in question. A third journal, which accepted the manuscript, was chosen partly on our guess that this same person would not again be one of the reviewers!"

Fourth, Glenn (1976) proposes that authors be allowed to prepare a reply to reviewers' comments on their paper before final disposition by the journal editorial board. This procedure might increase the length of the review time, but not by a great deal, since we could expect the author to respond quickly to the reviewers' comments in order to expedite the decision-making process. Currently, the only point where appeal is available is after the final decision has been communicated to the author—after the board has gone on record with its decision. Glenn (1976, p. 184) writes, "The purpose of this procedure would not be to involve the referees and authors in debates on minute and debatable points but rather to give the authors a chance to point out flagrant factual errors in the critiques, or provide valid and convincing counterarguments to poorly reasoned criticisms." Such a policy would have the additional effect of making editors more careful in their reviews.

Fifth, complementary to the fourth proposal is the recent policy of AJS and journals of the ASA of providing all reviewers of a given paper with the other reviewers' comments. This policy of circulating reviewers' comments to all reviewers has had, according to Glenn (1976), an important educational influence on reviewers. Although sharing reviewers' comments would be somewhat costly and time consuming, it would reduce intrusion of bias into the review process and make reviewers more careful in their review assignments. If there is intense disagreement among reviewers, it might be useful to publish the controversial paper along with the reviewers' comments, and let the scientific community judge. Intense disagreement may indicate that something important, even if faulty, is being said. If critical reviewers' comments are published along with the controversial paper, then the traditional authority bestowed by the act of publishing would be partly withdrawn and the reader left to make his or her own judgment. The added effort involved in the circulation of reviewers' comments would seem to be more than offset by the potential gains, and I recommend it. Mahoney (1977) has indicated that the journal *Cognitive Therapy and Research* will from time to time publish reviewers' comments. Ideally, all the procedures suggested here would be tested under experimental conditions to determine if, in fact, they do lead to improved manuscript review proceedings.

Sixth, it is not entirely clear what criteria journals use in the selection of members for the editorial board. Are those appointed the most accomplished scientists available? Are they selected because of their past performance in editorial review? Or are they selected because they are known by the editor? It is incumbent on journals to publish the procedures they follow in selecting editorial board members. There should be affirmative action to recruit all qualified scientists. Journals should be held accountable for the integrity of their recruitment procedures.

The positions should not be filled by friends and associates or those of like mind, but in accordance with a published set of criteria.

Seventh, one final recommendation. I have been tempted to write a chapter on author appeal procedures in the scientific publication system. The chapter heading would be followed by an empty space; on the next page, the following chapter would begin (see Upper, 1974). There is a dearth of discussion or apparent concern with author appeal procedures in the literature, with the exception of Glenn's proposal above. Yet, as Glenn (1976, p. 181) has asked, "Who knows how many persons have failed to receive tenure, promotions, and pay raises because of patently unfair rejections of their papers; or how many young sociologists have given up aspirations to be productive researchers or scholars after a few experiences with the vagaries of the review process; or how many papers which could have had an important impact on the discipline lie buried and neglected in obscure journals; or how many incorrect conclusions published in major journals have found their way into textbooks to be taught to unwary undergraduates or have influenced personal and policy decisions!" To protect against these problems, journals ought to establish formal author appeal procedures. There are a variety of forms these appeal procedures might take. I shall sketch one possible approach here; further study and experimentation is needed.

If an author believes that his or her submitted manuscript has been unfairly rejected, then (1) the author would prepare an appeal based on specific concerns with the reviewers' comments; (2) the reviewers would prepare a reply to the author's statement; (3) the appeal documents, along with the manuscript and the original reviews, would be reviewed by an impartial panel to decide whether there is justification for resubmitting the manuscript; and (4) if the panel deems it reasonable, the author would be allowed to resubmit the manuscript and have the previous reviews voided.

This appeal apparatus could be established by the professional associations such as the ASA, APA, and the National Association of Social Workers, and staffed by these organizations as a service to the journals. An appeal apparatus would increase the conscientiousness of the reviewer by alerting him or her that the author is not without recourse and may initiate action if a paper is not treated fairly (McCartney, 1978). Of course, the author always has the right to submit to another journal, but that does not obviate the need for procedural safeguards. Having an appeal system will allow the author to exercise his or her conscience when a matter of principle is involved. Furthermore, reviewers will be aware of this appeal procedure and thus be more careful in their judgments.

Conclusion

I present these analyses and recommendations in the hope of encouraging social and behavioral scientists actively to seek to improve the fairness and precision of the manuscript review process. Since the decisions of journal editorial boards are so vital to the health of science, I hope these suggestions may be used as a springboard for careful and systematic efforts to improve the operations of the journal publication system in the social and behavioral sciences.

8

Scientific Publication: Summary

————————

I am going to talk in an area that is not easy to address. But I believe that the issue and the charge of unfair reviewing is too important to be dissuaded by uneasiness. One problem for inquiry is the occurrence of emotional polarization. Every professional has vested interest in the publishing process, which makes self-justification more likely than impartial communication. Data is difficult to collect, as it requires cooperation in the release of materials which may not reflect favorably on professional performance.

—Spencer, 1978, p. 2

At this juncture, I would like to review what has been said and to indicate some limitations of the data and arguments of the preceding chapters. Professional journals serve the need of science to disseminate information. From their beginnings, they took on the responsibility of protecting the scientific literature from charlatans, quacks, and the unqualified by screening out inadequate material, and to bring the scholar and scientist into the wide network of professional colleagues through the rapid dissemination and critical exchange of ideas.

Professional journals have come to place less emphasis on their responsibility as a medium for critical inquiry. Instead, critical analysis is often shunned, and emphasis is placed on industrious work to extend dominant paradigms. This emphasis reifies a false image of science as removed from discord. The critical, the controversial, the imaginative are not allowed to see the light of day. To the extent that the professional journals do not encourage controversial work, the spirit of science has been diminished.

Chapter Three examined data from a survey of journal editors regarding their values in assessing a manuscript submitted for publication. The data indicate a divergence in methodological views among the editors and across the disciplines. However, the usefulness of these data must be questioned. The data are from a self-report survey, and the editors may simply be stating what they think ought to be the criteria, rather than what their criteria really are. Even the value of knowing these criteria is questionable: Editors can agree on the criteria, but when it comes to passing judgment there are considerable variations in the application of the criteria. Editors may apply the same criteria to the same paper and come up with widely divergent judgments. Nonetheless, collecting self-reports is a necessary first step in examining the normative criteria.

Chapter Four argued that there was a great deal of imprecision in the manuscript review process. The data suggested that the review process performs only a little better than random chance in assessing the "true quality" of a manuscript. This finding is quite discouraging. The review mechanism is apparently little able to differentiate the good from the bad paper. Nonetheless, the professional journals in the social and behavioral sciences reject about 80 percent of the papers they receive for lack of space to publish them all.

There are no doubt some problems with the probabilistic model of the journal review process. For one, the distribution of true quality may not be Gaussian (or normal). Nonetheless, it is suggestive of the imprecision that characterizes reviewers' judgments. What is the reason for this imprecision? Isn't the matter of differentiating a publishable manuscript straightforward? There are several possible explanations. First, it could be simply that there is a wide spectrum of possible "correct" judgments. Judges of beauty or goodness will likewise make plausible but differing assessments. The imprecision might also reflect the lack of consensus in the social and behavioral sciences regarding what is important, appropriate methodology, critical issues to be tackled, and so on. In some of the physical and biosciences, there is a relatively high consensus on these issues, but in the social and behavioral sciences there is a great deal of disagreement. It may also be that nonscientific criteria influence the review process. Since the manuscript review process is conducted in confidentiality, it is difficult to learn if nonscientific criteria are, in fact, influencing it.

Since it is difficult to determine what criteria actually operate, the next question is, "Who makes the decisions?" The data in Chapter Four suggest that in psychology and sociology the editors are distinguished contributors to their field. However, several of the national social work journals are staffed by individuals who have never published but who occupy editorial positions as a result of their administrative positions in social welfare agencies. Although an administrative position reflects success in the world of practice and there are, unfortunately, few other career options open to the successful social work practitioner, it should be kept in mind that administrator–editors could have a conservative influence on the nature of the literature published. Further, it is still an open question whether individuals who have never published an article in their professional careers should be in positions of judgment on the publishability of the manuscripts of others.

Chapter Five argued that even editorial board members who are distinguished contributors to their field may be so immersed in their own ongoing research that they have no time to review manuscripts submitted to the journal. The findings here are straightforward: Not all board members review the same number of manuscripts. The elite members of the editorial board often allow their names to appear on the masthead of the journal, lending prestige and authority to the journal and its contents while less prestigious members do most of the reviewing. It is primarily in psychology that the practice clearly is to appoint members for the prestige they can bring to the journal, not for the review services they can render. This does not hold true for the sociology journals studied. For the social work journals, the practice operates in reverse: The most distinguished members of the review boards are the most actively involved.

I question the integrity of the policy of appointing individuals to editorial review boards for the prestige they bring. There are better ways to confer prestige on eminent scientists than to appoint them as figureheads. Further, such a policy robs the review boards of needed assistance in the very important and demanding process of selecting which papers to publish. Finally, such an appointment pattern unfairly allocates credit to prestigious individuals while taking credit away from those who actually provide review services. In social work, where the most distinguished members of the board also do most of the reviewing, other individuals may be appointed to achieve an apparent balance of sex, race, and region—but their services are not used.

In Chapter Six, the angle of inquiry shifted from the editorial board to the product of the editorial review process— the published article. The discussion was broadened to include the fields of economics, psychiatry, and biochemistry. A sample of articles published in these fields in 1970 was examined in detail. The differences across fields were quite revealing. In psychology and biochemistry, articles are short; in sociology and economics, they are long. Almost all of the articles in biochemistry incorporate quantitative analysis, whereas less than 20 percent of those in the applied fields of social work and psychiatry incorporate such analysis. Three quarters of the articles in biochemistry (nearly all if foreign authors were not included) acknowledged grant funding, whereas in the social and behavioral sciences less than half, and in the applied sciences of social work and psychiatry less than a quarter, of the articles acknowledged grant funding.

There is more money to support publication in biochemistry as a result of the policy of charging page fees conditioned on grant funding. Since most of the articles acknowledge grant funds, they essentially pay for their own publishing. The rejection rates of about 20 to 30 percent in biochemistry are much lower than in the social and behavioral sciences. It has been argued that the lower rejection rates in the physical and biological sciences may reflect the greater paradigm consensus in these fields, while in the social sciences lack of agreement on central problems, adequate methodology, and so on, results in higher rejection rates. However, I believe that controversy and the absence of consensus should not lead to higher rejection rates but to a livelier dialogue. Dissensus leads to higher rejection rates only if professional journals have abandoned their concern with fostering criticism and scholarly inquiry, which it appears they have.

Keep in mind, however, that journal editors and their review boards respond to journal space limitations when they reject 80 percent of the papers submitted. In the social sciences, there is less money to sponsor publication efforts. With limited funding, social and behavioral science review boards have only published what they have funds to support. Over the years, the response to financial contingencies has come to be viewed as a choice or option elected by review boards. They publish only what is consensually assessed as good and return the rest. Yet, if more space were available, the habits of reviewers would change, and more manuscripts would be published. The result would be greater critical discussion and analysis.

In biochemistry, I estimated that there are about three article spaces (and more than six authorship spaces) yearly per working scientist. This guarantees the working biochemist that he or she will be able to publish whatever is written up. There is no such guarantee in the social and behavioral sciences. In fact, because of the substantial imprecision in the review process, even good papers are not assured of publication. This bottleneck in the publication system not only limits the opportunity of the submitting author but in the long run also deprives the field of substantial contributions.

The articles published in the various fields are quite different in terms of the age of the literature they build on. For biochemistry most of the literature used in articles comes from recent publications. This gives the literature an ability to move quickly in a given problem area. In contrast, the literature in the social and behavioral sciences is built on a more established foundation. The articles used in constructing a new article are older and longer. Rather than contributing to a rapidly moving research front, the articles in the social and behavioral sciences are more concerned with enduring contributions that advance theory through reformulation rather than empirical tests.

Chapter Seven critically examined the manuscript review process, taking into account both previous studies and the findings reported in the earlier chapters. The chapter indicated that there is a confirmatory bias among reviewers; that is, they tend to support publication of papers that are in conformity with their own views and to reject papers that contradict their own methodological or theoretical views. In view of the imprecision in the review process and high rejection rates, these experimental research findings are quite discouraging.

One of the distinguishing characteristics of articles published in the prestigious journals is that their authors come from the elite universities (Wanderer, 1966; Lin and Nelson, 1969; Prescott and Csikszentmihalyi, 1977). This is puzzling in light of the data reported in Chapter Six indicating that author characteristics were insignificant in predicting the number of citations an article would attract over a seven-year period after its publication. The imprecision in the review process makes this even more puzzling—unless, of course, those in elite universities dominate in terms of the number of submissions. I have no data on this. However, the Prescott and Csikszentmihalyi study (1977) indicates that authors with prestigious affiliations do not dominate the less prestigious journals. Their data indicate that the prestige of the journal is roughly equal to its proportion of authors from prestigious institutions.

What we have in the manuscript review process, then, is a sieve that is supposed to filter out inadequate contributions. However, when the sieve is tested its ability to discriminate is quite limited, if not wholly lacking. Pfeffer, Salancik, and Leblebici (1976) warn that in situations where objective criteria are missing, particularistic standards are likely to appear. Particularistic standards, such as university affiliation and previous accomplishments, enter into the editorial review decision. As it is now, one wonders how much chance an author from Delta State

College, for example, has in publishing the results of his or her inquiry, no matter how promising, in a prestigious journal.

This rather bleak picture is in large measure a result of the bottleneck in the social and behavioral science publication system. If all were entitled to publish their views, irrespective of their affiliation, status, or paradigmatic commitment, and be held responsible through a system of letters to the editor and so forth, then the stifling of unpopular or critical views would be much less.

One of the distinguishing characteristics of the social and behavioral science editorial review proceeding is the length of the review process. The typical article probably waits in the review and publication queue more than two years before publication. In contrast, in the physical sciences the review and publication queue moves rapidly. Articles are accepted and published rapidly. They are quickly picked up and used by other investigators for subsequent research, creating the opportunity for a rapidly moving research front. The emphasis is on contributing new findings, not on producing an enduring scholarly contribution. In brief, the journal publication system facilitates and is partly responsible for the character of research in different fields. In the social sciences, the current structure of the journal review process restricts entry to the most current research front to those with access to preprints from active researchers (Hagstrom, 1970; Crane, 1972).

In biochemistry, the reinforcement for productive effort operates effectively. When a scientist conducts some research and writes it up, he or she is virtually assured publication. The publication of the work reinforces the research behavior, encouraging the biochemist to engage in additional research. The reinforcement process is not as effective in the social and behavioral sciences. Here an investigator may spend considerable time and effort in conducting a study only to learn that it is not acceptable in the current competitive conditions.

It is important to note that in the social and behavioral sciences rejection is not by a simple form rejection letter, but usually involves a lengthy discourse on the problems of the paper. The provision of extensive reviewers' comments is an important educational service. However, it is punishing to be rejected, even if one is in a large pool of rejectees. The consequences of this punishment on subsequent behavior may be more harmful to science than is usually recognized.

I have been arguing that a number of compounding problems accrue to the social and behavioral sciences as a result of restricted publication opportunities. Perhaps most serious is the intrusion of particularistic and nonscientific standards into the review proceedings. It is of the utmost importance for the morale of the field to protect against these biases. Little attention has been given to this matter, in order not to create the appearance of questioning the integrity of editors. But it is not the integrity of editors that is in question. Substantial evidence from the field of experimental social psychology indicates that individuals are just not aware of the extent to which particularistic standards influence their cognitive and judgmental processes. In the highly restrictive publication conditions that exist in the social and behavioral sciences, it is essential that authors believe they are having a fair and impartial review. Many authors are not having such a review and are aware of it (Brackbill and Korten, 1970). This is not because of the tainted intentions of reviewers, who do a great deal of onerous work for a pittance of prestige, but because of the ineffective regulatory mechanisms built into the review process.

I believe greater attention should be paid to the need for effective author appeal procedures. Such procedures would not be a catastrophe tying the profession up in endless disputes over decisions. The mechanisms for author appeals that are needed do not have to do with the validity of the final judgment but with the process by which it was derived. The appeal mechanisms and reforms recommended in Chapter Seven would ensure that the process was as fair and honest as possible.

High-quality science comes from an atmosphere of high integrity. The social and behavioral sciences are vulnerable to the decline of morale because of low paradigm development and very competitive conditions. I sense that over the years the critical edge that is so essential to the vitality of these fields has been declining, in no small measure because of the conditions

outlined in this book. The creative, questioning spirit that pene-
trates and reveals has been exchanged by aspiring social and
behavioral scientists for the dogged pursuit of knowledge in the
computer printout. The wind of dustbowl empiricism that C.
Wright Mills (1959) cautioned against blows strongly under these
conditions. The proper design and analysis of a set of empirical
data bearing on some narrow topic is less subject to criticism:
The paradigm is clear, the consensus on standards high. However, the contribution that results from these endless hours of
searching for significant correlations and other statistical indi-
cators can be questioned. I fear that the current conditions of
the publication system in the social and behavioral sciences have
given rise to a generation of scholars and scientists who view the
computer, statistical models, and an absence of concern with
the moral and political questions of the day as the requisite
materials for building a successful career.

The best defense against these trends is a scientific publication system that takes seriously its responsibility to foster a
critical attitude. This will require the implementation of policies
that ensure that the critical edge is not honed down through an
overly competitive and imprecise review process. It will also
require greater attention to the limitations imposed by the
publication system, so that the system itself will not limit the
vitality and contribution of the social and behavioral sciences it
is meant to serve.

Measurement Note : Assessing Quality in Science

―――――――――――――――

It is possible to rank order all 100,000 social scientists three times a year. For an individual to move from, say, 85,274th most cited social scientist in May, to the 67,319th in December, would be an indication of intellectual growth and increasing status, a reason to go out to dinner, if not to ask for a promotion. . . . One imagines the eventual establishment of a social science ticker tape, which would spread citation rates to the offices of deans and department chairmen instantaneously. (A burst of noise from the ticker; the dean rushes over and reads off the spattering tape, "Daniel Bell up 6.")
                                                                    —Wiener, 1977, p. 174

Early studies of the social system of science were restricted to assessing the contribution of a scientist by a simple count of the scientist's publications. The limitation of this quantitative assessment was recognized (Manis, 1951). However, the alternative of introducing an assessment of the quality of each published manuscript seemed to pose insurmountable difficulties. Who was to judge? In one of the very few studies to provide individual assessment of each publication, Shaw (1967) had the scientists themselves assess their own work. In the most refined

128

measures, the quality of each published manuscript was assessed by evaluating the prestige of the journal in which it appeared (Glenn and Villemez, 1970).

   With the advent of citation indices, the picture in the sociology of science has changed. Hargens (1975, p. 87) observes, "The single most important technical development behind the growth and interest in the sociology of science has been the emergence of practical means to measure the quantity and quality of a scientist's published work. . . . Primarily responsible for the development of these measures is the *Science Citation Index.*" The logic of citation counts is simple: If an author's work is of value it will be used by others. To illustrate, if a scientist published two papers in a given year and one of them received twenty-five citations and the other two citations during the same period, it would be reasonable to assert that the former paper was of higher quality than the latter. Citation counts have the additional advantage of being less subject to personal manipulation. Further, validation studies have consistently indicated that citation counts correlate quite highly with such other measures of quality as location in a prestigious university, being listed in important bibliographies of scientists, receiving scientific awards, and recognition by colleagues (Myers, 1970; Quandt, 1976; Zuckerman, 1977).

   Citation counts have also served as a useful indicator of the cumulative knowledge in various specialty areas and fields (Menard, 1971; Crane, 1972). If the work occurring in a given field is leading to a cumulative body of knowledge, then reference trails among the work of the contributors will be left in the form of citations (Mullins, 1973, 1975; Cole, 1976). Study of the knowledge base in various fields has often focused on the cumulative growth of knowledge (Freese, 1972; Parsons, 1954).

   I have used citation counts in my studies of the operation of the publication system in science and found them a quite useful indicator. However, after several years of using this measure, I have increasingly come to question its utility as a robust measure of *quality*. Although it may be the most convenient and reasonable measure available, it is not without serious shortcomings that need to be examined in order that results derived using this measure can be put in proper perspective. In this discussion, I shall propose alternative ways of interpreting citation counts and then explore some of the shortcomings of the citation count. My aim is not to discourage use of citation counts but rather to encourage their use with caution and perhaps with refinements suggested by the following critique. Even if I am unduly critical, the balance will be proper, since the thrust of previous studies has been overly enthusiastic.

Citation Counts: The Scientific Nielsen Rating

For a number of years, television broadcasting companies have relied on the Nielsen ratings for assessing the popularity and appeal of network programs. In essence, the Nielsen ratings estimate the number and type of people who watch a particular program. The agency that distributes the Nielsen ratings makes no pretense that they are a measure of quality (Nielsen, 1964). In fact, the Nielsen ratings are not a measure of quality programming (Cantor, 1971; Meyers, 1962). I do not know what the correlation between the Nielsen ratings and the presentation of Emmy Awards is, but I suspect it would be around the same as would be found between citation counts and a "true" measure of scientific quality. Yet, just as the Nielsen ratings are a useful, if not always accurate, indicator for sorting between good and bad programs (few people will continue to watch a dull program), so also are citation counts useful in sorting between good and bad papers. It is this characteristic of citation counts that has justified their use as a measure of quality.

Citation counts can, in large measure, be viewed as the Nielsen ratings of science. Citation counts tell us the extent to which a publication is being read. Just as the 1,200 families in the Nielsen sample record the programs they watch on an audimeter, so scientists acknowledge on the reference lists of their manuscripts the publications they have read. However, not all publications that are read are then cited; it is this distinction that gives the citation count its unique character. If an article presents a major contribution or a significant error, it will probably be cited more frequently than another paper. Yet, the allocation of citations is something we know little about (Chubin and Moitra, 1975; Dieks and Chang, 1976; Moravcsik and Murugesan, 1975). Crane (1972, p. 20) writes, "Little is known about how scientists decide to cite papers in their work and presumably not all citations in a particular paper have contributed equally to its contents."

What is it then, that citations counts tell us? They tell us a great deal about invisible colleges that form around scientific specialities (Mullins, 1973). Who is citing whom, what specialty groups are forming, whether conflicting research programs are emerging, and who has the greatest access to the publication system can be discerned from citation studies. This is information for studying the underlife of scientific communities that, paradoxically enough, has been relatively neglected in the mainstream sociology of science literature.

Stratification Studies in Science

Probably the most frequent use of citation counts has been in the study of the stratification system in science. In this context, citation counts have been used primarily as a measure of quality. Although citation counts have proven very useful in studying the social communication system in science, the use of citation counts to assess the quality of those communications may stretch their utility too far.

Anomalous Findings

Working with citation counts, anomalies constantly arise. How is it that important scientific work is often unrecognized long after it is published? Polanyi's article on the "potential theory of absorption" went uncited for twenty-five years because it contradicted the consensus of the major scientists of the time (see Holton, 1978, for other examples of delayed recognition). Then there is the problem of popularized drivel that receives many citations. The question might be asked as to which of Blalock's books is more important: *Social Statistics* (1960) or *Causal Inferences in Nonexperimental Research* (1964). According to citation counts, it is the *Social Statistics* textbook, by almost twice as much. Nevertheless, his study on causal inference with correlational data is certainly viewed by the scientific community as his most important methodological work (Mullins, 1975).

Griffith and Small (1976) created a cumulative file from the *Social Science Citation Index* (SSCI) for the years 1972 to 1974 and identified those documents cited more than 200 times. The list is most revealing. The two most cited items are elementary statistics texts. This finding tells us more about the state of the social sciences than the quality and importance of these documents. The texts are Winer's *Statistical Principles in Experimental Design* (1962) and Siegal's *Non-Parametric Statistics for the Behavioral Sciences* (1956) with 1,333 and 1,020 citations respectively. After these documents, there is a sharp drop to the third most cited item—Osgood, Suci, and Tannenbaum's *Measurement of Meaning* (1957), with 480 citations. What these findings suggest is that when social scientists use a popular statistic they feel compelled to cite the elementary statistic text from which they learned it.

Although citation counts are apparently unable to distinguish quality among methodological contributions, as the example of Blalock's work illustrates, there is the puzzling finding that methodological and statistical contributions consistently have high citation counts. In the social sciences at least, it would be fair to ask if compilations of useful statistical procedures in textbook form, or new mathematical or statistical models, are the major contributions that citation counts suggest they are. Unquestionably, methodological and statistical contributions are important, but their value seems much overestimated by citation counts.

In the physical and biosciences, methodological and instrumentational contributions predominate in attracting citations. Garfield (1977) has constructed a listing of the 249 most cited documents from the *Science Citation Index*. The most highly cited document is "Protein Measurement with the Folin Phenol Reagent" by Lowry and others (1951), with more than 50,000 citations! This citation count is nearly seven times larger than the next item on the list. When queried about the importance of this paper, Lowry suggested that it was not his best paper. Even if citation counts are useful in the natural sciences for identifying valuable methodology and instrumentation contributions, these are not necessarily synonomous with quality.

The most highly cited item appearing since 1970 in the Griffith and Small (1976) study was Alvin Toffler's *Future Shock* (1970), with 268 citations. It should be noted that the sources of these citations are the professional and scholarly journals used by the Institute for Scientific Information in building the SSCI. Although Toffler's contribution had only recently arrived on the scene, it attracted almost as many citations as the most highly cited sociological document on the list, Merton's classic, *Social Theory and Social Structure* (1957), with 313 citations.

One of the more popular sociological theorists in the late 1960s and early 1970s was Marshall McLuhan. I have examined the "quality" of his work as assessed by the citation indexes from 1969 to 1976 (see Table 21). One difficulty with this examination was that the SSCI increased its coverage each year during this period; thus the citation counts for a document would appear to be increasing, even if its true measure, standardized by year, were stable. The finding that the impact of McLuhan's work declined systematically from 1969 to 1976 conservatively estimates the extent of the decline. In the cases of both McLuhan and Toffler, we have an illustration of the Nielsen-rating character of citation counts.

The Cognitive Element of Science

Contributions to knowledge have an essential cognitive and intellectual core that is not directly assessed by citation counts. Although assessment of this core is essential, there is no compelling logical reason why citation counts should be sensitive

TABLE 21.   Distribution of Citations to the Work of Marshall McLuhan.

Year	Number of Citations
1969	102
1970	85
1971	94
1972	69
1973	42
1974	52
1975	65
1976	50

to it. At their best, citation counts provide a crude, indirect, unobtrusive indicator of the quality of a contribution's cognitive and intellectual core. This feature of citation counts touches on a point that will be examined later, namely, that citation counts are biased toward the logical positivism of the hard sciences and away from the scholarship of the arts and humanities. While this may not be a severe problem when assessing work in the natural and physical sciences (although it is a problem there too—see Holton, 1973), it becomes a critical deficiency in assessing social science contributions.

Sorting the Extremes

Citation counts are probably reasonably good for sorting the extreme ends of the continuum on the dimension of the quality of scientific work. Yet even here, as the preceding examples illustrate, they have limitations. In the middle range of the continuum of quality, citation counts are of doubtful utility.

This can be seen by examining the distribution of citations to the cohort of articles from several fields discussed in Chapter Six. The cumulative frequency distributions for the separate fields reveal that a few documents attract most of the citations (see Figure 4). Across all fields, the top 10 percent of the most cited articles attract between 42 and 49 percent of all citations within their respective fields. What is evident is that most articles

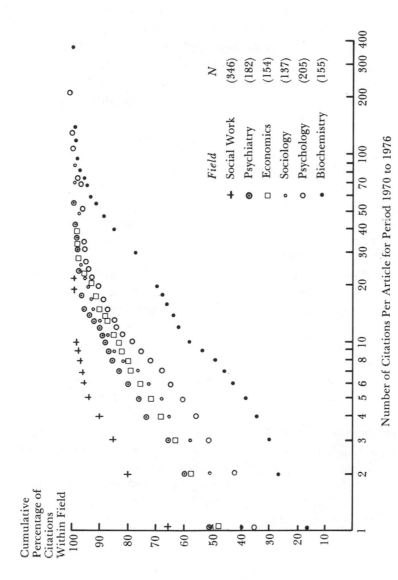

Cumulative
Percentage of
Citations
Within Field

Field		N
+	Social Work	(346)
◉	Psychiatry	(182)
□	Economics	(154)
∘	Sociology	(137)
○	Psychology	(205)
●	Biochemistry	(155)

Number of Citations Per Article for Period 1970 to 1976

FIGURE 4. Cumulative Distribution of Citations to Articles by Field.

are rarely cited, while a few attract an extraordinary number of citations.

Figure 4 shows that the cumulative distribution of citations fits a straight line when plotted on semilog graph paper. That is, the cumulative citations appear to follow a log function for every field, at least through the middle of the distribution, where the log function then breaks down. The distributions are all asymptotic in the upper tails. Since it is the documents in the upper tails that receive a majority of the citations, it is hard to discount their departure from the logistic model (see Price, 1965). It might be possible to develop a more precise description of the distribution that would more accurately account for a greater number of points, including those in the tails. Nonetheless, it is obvious that in the middle of the distribution the difference between articles is relatively minor. The difference between the article that attracts no citations and the one that attracts three over a seven-year period does not seem substantial (Cole and Cole, 1973). Yet, for all fields except biochemistry, more than half of the articles fall within this limited range. Eliminating psychology, this range is reduced to between zero and two. For the applied fields of psychiatry and social work, it is reduced to between zero and one.

These data suggest that in fields where scientists write few papers citation counts may be a very gross measure of the quality of scientific contributions to knowledge (Wolff, 1970). In the natural and physical sciences, where there is extensive publication and the distribution of citations appears to be more spread, citations might serve as a more useful *variable* for assessing an article's quality. The distribution of citations to articles in this cohort of literature suggests the need to examine the overall distribution of citations for a sample of scientists, and thus to ensure that there is a spread before citation counts are used to differentiate the quality of the contribution of sample members.

Critical Reflections on Citations

It would be highly desirable in the empirical study of social systems of science to have a machine that could sort out and efficiently evaluate the quality of scientific work. This quality-sensor machine would greatly facilitate empirical studies in the sociology of science. Reading the literature in the area, one gets the impression that such an evaluation machine exists. Cole and Cole (1973, p. 21) write, "The invention of the *Science Citation Index* a few years ago provides a new tool which we believe yields a reliable and valid measure of the significance of individual scientists' contributions." Kochen and Perkel (1977, p. 1) go further: "The quality of a paper is interpreted primarily as a likelihood of its being appropriately cited. Analysis of these algorithms leads to interesting research problems, such as the possibility of nonsubjective measures of quality by the use of modified cocitation counts." In reading the literature in the sociology of science, one finds that authors talking about citations shift to citation counts as measures of quality and then to discussions of quality, on the assumption that quality is determined by a count of citations. This shift from metaphor to myth is similar to what occurred in the field of mental health. In the early years of the insane asylums and mental hospitals, the inmates' problems were discussed "as if" they were mental diseases. The "as if" was soon dropped; to this day, psychiatrists talk about "mental diseases," even though the empirical evidence has not come in (Sarbin, 1972; Rosenthal, 1970; Scheff, 1966). Maybe it is early enough in our study of the sociology of science to caution against the dropping of the "as if" when discussing whether citations measure quality.

Esthetic Criticism and the Citation Count. The limitations of logical positivism have been most clear in the realm of the social sciences. The normative model of the sociology of science is a sociology of the natural and physical sciences (Mulkay, 1976; Rothman, 1972). The normative tradition is itself informed by logical positivism (Law, 1974). Theorists from the Frankfurt School have been an important source of criticism of the "popularity and appeal" of logical positivism in the modern social sciences (Jay, 1973). The critical theorists caution that positivism attempts to enshrine facts in a manner that is not possible in the cultural and social sciences. Within the positivistic paradigm, facts are given a separate-from-subject quality (Cunningham, 1973); that is, an objectivity that can be assessed without reference to the subject. In the case of citation counts, this suggests they can be used to distinguish the quality of a contribution to science without reference to subjective assessment. Yet it must be remembered that a citation represents the subjective assessment of the citer.

Ethical and Political Dimensions of Quality. Poole (1972, p. 12) has observed, "A fault has occurred in our reason. One half of our modern rationality has dropped sheerly away, leaving the cliff face of scientific and political objectivity towering uselessly over the void. . . . The strata of reason, thus violently sundered, continue at a lower level, but they are unrecognizable from above. Objectivity has been deserted, left high and exposed by subjectivity." To be meaningful to human society, to be useful to the effort of creating a more humane and democratic social order, social science has to be deeply sensitive to ethical and political considerations (Becker, 1967). Social and behavioral science research is, in contrast to physical and natural science research, an effort to integrate ethical and value concerns with the inquisitive search for knowledge (Lynn, [1938] 1964). These several components cannot be separated and examined independently without destroying their delicate connective tissue. In fact, it is the ethical, moral, and political issues that have guided the scientist's development of a particular social science contribution and that form its esthetic and subjective quality.

The positivistic view, which informs the normative model of science, neglects the involvement of the subject. The definition of quality in terms of citation counts illustrates this—in the process of counting citations, the observer does not exercise subjective judgment and consequently attempts to assess the quality of science without reference to ethical or political questions. However, the objective observation and measurement of phenomena alone do not result in the development of knowledge (Polanyi, 1958). The effort of reason and understanding, which can only be accomplished by a subject, is the effort of science. Critically analyzing and assessing possibilities characterize the development of knowledge, especially in the social sciences.

At this juncture, the conservative orientation of logical

Ben-David, J. "The Profession of Science and Its Powers." *Minerva*, 1972, *10*, 362–383.

Benedik, E. P. "Editorial Practices of Psychiatric and Related Journals: Implications for Women." *American Journal of Psychiatry*, 1976, *133*, 89–92.

Berg, S. V. "Structure, Behavior, and Performance in the Scientific Journal Market." Unpublished doctoral dissertation, Yale University, 1970.

Bernal, J. D. *The Social Function of Science*. London: Routledge & Kegan Paul, 1939.

Bernstein, I. N., and Freeman, H. E. *Academic and Entrepreneurial Research*. New York: Russell Sage Foundation, 1975.

Blalock, H. M., Jr. *Social Statistics*. New York: McGraw-Hill, 1960.

Blalock, H. M., Jr. *Causal Inferences in Nonexperimental Research*. Chapel Hill: University of North Carolina Press, 1964.

Blalock, H. M., Jr. (Ed.). *Causal Models in the Social Sciences*. Chicago: Aldine, 1971.

Blalock, H. M., Jr. "Can We Find a Genuine Ordinal Slope Analogue?" In D. R. Heise (Ed.), *Sociological Methodology 1976*. San Francisco: Jossey-Bass, 1975.

Blau, P. M. *The Organization of Academic Work*. New York: Wiley, 1973.

Blume, S. S. *Toward a Political Sociology of Science*. New York: Free Press, 1974.

Books in Print. Vol. 1.: *Authors*. New York: Bowker, 1974.

Boor, M. "Unfamiliarity Breeds Disdain: Comment on Department Chairpersons' Ratings of Psychological Journals." *American Psychologist*, 1973, *28*, 1012–1013.

Bowen, D. D., Perloff, R., and Jacoby, J. "Improving Manuscript Evaluation Procedures." *American Psychologist*, 1972, *27*, 221–225.

Brackbill, Y., and Korten, F. "Journal Reviewing Practices: Authors' and APA Members' Suggestions for Revision." *American Psychologist*. 1970, *25*, 937–940.

Bronowski, J. *The Ascent of Man*. Boston: Little, Brown, 1973.

Burton, R. E., and Kebler, R. W., "The 'Half-Life' of Some Scientific and Technical Literature." *American Documentation*, 1960, *11*, 18–22.

Buss, A. R., and McDermott, J. R. "Ratings of Psychology Journals Compared to Objective Measures of Journal Impact." *American Psychologist*, 1976, *31*, 675–678.

Cantor, M. F. *The Hollywood TV Producer.* New York: Basic Books, 1971.

Chase, J. "Normative Criteria for Scientific Publication." *American Sociologist*, 1970, *5*, 262–265.

Chubin, D. "The Use of Science Citation Index in Sociology." *American Sociologist*, 1973, *8*, 187–189.

Chubin, D. E., and Moitra, S. D. "Content Analysis of References: Adjunct or Alternative to Citation Counting?" *Social Studies of Science*, 1975, *5*, 423–441.

Cicourel, A. V. *Method and Measurement in Sociology.* New York: Free Press, 1964.

Clark, C. X. "Introduction: Some Reflexive Comments on the Role of Editor." *Journal of Social Issues*, 1973, *29* (1), 1–9.

Clasquin, F. F., and Cohen, J. B. "Prices of Physics and Chemistry Journals." *Science*, 1977, *197*, 432–438.

Cole, J. R., and Cole, S. "The Ortega Hypothesis." *Science*, 1972, *178*, 368–375.

Cole, J., and Cole, S. *Social Stratification in Science.* Chicago: University of Chicago Press, 1973.

Cole, S. "The Growth of Scientific Knowledge: Theories of Deviance as a Case Study." In L. Coser (Ed.), *The Idea of Social Structure.* New York: Harcourt Brace Jovanovich, 1976.

Costner, H. L., and Leik, R. K. "Deductions from Axiomatic Theory." *American Sociological Review*, 1964, *29*, 819–835.

Cournand, A., and Meyer, M. "The Scientist's Code." *Minerva*, 1976, *14*, 79–96.

Cox, E. P., Hamelman, P. W., and Wilcox, J. B. "Relational Characteristics of the Business Literature: An Interpretive Procedure." *The Journal of Business*, 1976, *49*, 252–265.

Crandall, R. "*How* Qualified are Editors?" *American Psychologist*, 1977, *32*, 5.

Crandall, R. "Interrater Agreement on Manuscripts Is Not So Bad!" *American Psychologist*, in press.

Crane, D. "Scientists at Major Universities." *American Sociological Review*, 1965, *30*, 699–714.

Crane, D. "The Gatekeepers of Science: Some Factors Affecting the Selection of Articles for Scientific Journals." *American Sociologist*, 1967, *2*, 195-201.

Crane, D. *Invisible Colleges: Diffusion of Knowledge in Scientific Communities*. Chicago: University of Chicago Press, 1972.

Cunningham, F. *Objectivity in Social Science*. Toronto: University of Toronto Press, 1973.

Denzin, N. K. *The Research Act*. Chicago: Aldine, 1970.

Dieks, D., and Chang, H. "Differences in Impact of Scientific Publications: Some Indices Derived from a Citation Analysis." *Social Studies of Science*, 1976, *6*, 247-267.

Dillman, D., and others. "Increasing Mail Questionnaire Responses: A Four-State Comparison." *American Sociological Review*, 1974, *39*, 744-756.

Duncan, O. T. "Path Analysis: Sociological Examples." *American Journal of Sociology*, 1966, *72*, 1-16.

Duncan, O. T. *Introduction to Structural Equation Models*. New York: Academic Press, 1975.

Edge, D. O., and Mulkay, M. J. *Astronomy Transformed: The Emergence of Radio Astronomy in Britain*. New York: Wiley-Interscience, 1976.

Edwards, A. L. *An Introduction to Linear Regression and Correlation*. San Francisco: W. H. Freeman, 1976.

Else, J. F. "The State of Social Work Journal Publications: Patterns and Implications." *Social Work*, 1978, *23*, 267-273.

Fisher, C. S. "The Death of Mathematical Theory: A Study in the Sociology of Knowledge." *Archives for History of Exact Sciences*, 1966, *3*, 137-159.

Fisher, C. S. "The Last Invariant Theorists." *European Journal of Sociology*, 1967, *8*, 216-244.

Flexner, A. "Is Social Work a Profession?" Proceedings of the National Conference of Social Work, 42nd annual session, Baltimore, Md., May 12-19, 1915.

Fliedner, T. M. "Three 'C': A Challenge." *European Journal of Clinical Investigation*, 1976, *6*, 1-5.

Fores, M. "Price, Technology, and the Paper Model." *Technology and Culture*, 1971, *12*, 621-627.

Freese, L. "Cumulative Sociological Knowledge." *American Sociological Review*, 1972, *37*, 472-482.

Fruton, J. S. "The Emergence of Biochemistry." *Science*, 1976, *192*, 327–334.

Garfield, E. "Citation Analysis as a Tool in Journal Evaluation." *Science*, 1972, *178*, 471–479.

Garfield, E. "The 250 Most-Cited Primary Authors, 1961–1975. Part 3: Each Author's Most-Cited Publication." *Current Contents*, 1977, *51*, 5–20.

Germain, C. B. "Casework and Science: A Study in the Sociology of Knowledge." Unpublished doctoral dissertation, Columbia University, 1971.

Gilbert, G. N., and Woolgar, S. "The Quantitative Study of Science: An Examination of the Literature." *Science Studies*, 1974, *4*, 279–294.

Gilbert, N. "Editorial Board Membership." *American Psychologist*, 1977, *32*, 1109–1110.

Giles, M. W., and Wright, G. C. "Political Scientists' Evaluations of Sixty-Three Journals." *PS*, 1975, 254–256.

Glenn, N. D. "American Sociologists' Evaluations of Sixty-Three Journals." *American Sociologist*, 1971, *6*, 283–303.

Glenn, N. D. "The Journal Article Review Process: Some Proposals for Change." *American Sociologist*, 1976, *11*, 179–185.

Glenn, N. D. *Cohort Analysis*. Beverly Hills, Calif.: Sage, 1977.

Glenn, N. D. "Statement of the New Editor." *Contemporary Sociology*, 1978, 7, 5–6.

Glenn, N. D., and Villemez, W. "The Productivity of Sociologists in 45 American Universities." *American Sociologist*, 1970, *5*(2), 244–252.

Goudsmit, S. A. "It's Not Fair." *Physical Review Letters*, 1968, *21*, 1425.

Gouldner, A. W. *The Coming Crisis of Western Sociology*. New York: Basic Books, 1970.

Griffith, B., and Small, H. G. "A Philadelphia Study of the Structure of Science: The Structure of the Social and Behavioral Science Literature." Proceedings of the 1st International Conference on Social Studies of Science, Ithaca, N.Y., November 4–6, 1976.

Gustin, B. H. "Charisma, Recognition, and the Motivation of Scientists." *American Journal of Sociology*, 1973, *78* (5), 1119–1134.

Gynther, M. D. "On Mace and Warner's Journal Ratings." *American Psychologist*, 1973, *28*, 1013.

Hagstrom, W. "Factors Related to the Use of Different Modes of Publishing Research in Four Scientific Fields." In C. E. Nelson and D. K. Pollock (Eds.), *Communication Among Scientists and Engineers*. Lexington, Mass.: Heath, 1970.

Hamelman, P. W., and Mazze, E. M. "Toward a Cost/Utility Model for Social Science Periodicals." *Socio-Economic Planning Sciences*, 1972, *6*, 465-476.

Hamelman, P. W., and Mazze, E. M. "Measuring the Research Impact of Business Journals: The Casper Model." *Journal of Economics and Business*, 1973, *25*, 164-167.

Hargens, L. L. *Patterns of Scientific Research: A Comparative Analysis of Research in Three Scientific Fields*. Washington, D.C.: American Sociological Association, 1975.

Hargens, L. L., and Hagstrom, W. O. "Sponsored and Contest Mobility of American Academic Scientists." *Sociology of Education*, 1967, *40*, 24-38.

Hargens, L. L., Mullins, N. C., and Hecht, P. K. "Research Areas and Stratification Processes in Science." Unpublished paper, Department of Sociology, Indiana University, 1978.

Harman, H. *Modern Factor Analysis*. (2nd ed.) Chicago: University of Chicago Press, 1967.

Harris, R. J. *A Primer of Multivariate Statistics*. New York: Academic Press, 1975.

Hawkins, R. G., Ritter, L. S., and Walter, I. "What Economists Think of Their Journals." *The Journal of Political Economy*, 1973, *81*, 1017-1032.

Hendrick, C. "Editorial Comment." *Personality and Social Psychology Bulletin*, 1976, *2*, 207-208.

Hendrick, C. "Editorial Comment." *Personality and Social Psychology Bulletin*, 1977, *3*, 1.

Hohn, R. L., and Fine, J. J. "Ratings and Misratings: A Reply to Mace and Warner." *American Psychologist*, 1973, *28*, 1012.

Holton, G. *Thematic Origins of Scientific Thought*. Cambridge, Mass.: Harvard University Press, 1973.

Holton, G. "Can Science be Measured?" In Y. Elkana and others (Eds.), *Toward a Metric of Science*. New York: Wiley-Interscience, 1978.

Inhaber, H. "Is There a Pecking Order in Physics Journals?" *Physics Today*, 1974, *27*, 39-43.

Institute for Scientific Information. *Science Citation Index.* Philadelphia, Pa.: Institute for Scientific Information, 1970-1976.

Institute for Scientific Information. *Social Science Citation Index.* Philadelphia, Pa.: Institute for Scientific Information, 1969-1976.

Institute of Labor and Industrial Relations. *Poverty and Human Resource Abstracts.* Vols. 1-9. Beverly Hills, Calif.: Sage, 1966-1974.

Jay, M. *The Dialectical Imagination: A History of the Frankfurt School and the Institute of Social Research, 1923-50.* Boston: Little, Brown, 1973.

Kahn, A. (Ed.). *Shaping the New Social Work.* New York: Columbia University Press, 1973.

Kevles, D. J. *The Physicists: The History of a Scientific Community in America.* New York: Knopf, 1971.

Khinduka, S. K. "Editorial." *Journal of Social Service Research*, 1977, *1*, 3-4.

Kirk, S. A., Osmalov, M. J., and Fischer, J. "Social Workers' Involvement in Research." *Social Work*, 1976, *21*(2), 121-124.

Kochen, M., and Perkel, B. "Improving Referee-Selection and Manuscript Evaluation." In J. McCartney (Ed.), *Proceedings of the First International Conference of Scientific Editors.* Dordrecht, The Netherlands: Reidel, 1977.

Kochen, M., and Tagliacozzo, R. "Matching Authors and Readers of Scientific Papers." *Information Storage and Retrieval*, 1974, *10*, 197-210.

Koulack, D., and Kesselman, H. J. "Ratings of Psychology Journals by Members of the American Psychological Association." *American Psychologist*, 1975, *30*, 1049-1053.

Kroll, H. W. "Institutional Sources of Articles Published in Social Work Journals: 1965-1974." *Arete*, 1976, *4*, 121-125.

Kronick, D. A. *A History of Scientific and Technical Periodicals: The Origins and Development of the Scientific and Technical Press, 1665-1790.* Metuchen, N.J.: Scarecrow Press, 1976.

Kuhn, T. "The Function of Measurement in Modern Physical

Science." *ISIS*, 1961, *52*, 161–193.

Kuhn, T. S. *The Structure of Scientific Revolutions*. Chicago: University of Chicago Press, 1962.

Lane, M. "Books and Their Publishers." In J. Tunstall (Ed.), *Media Sociology*. Urbana: University of Illinois Press, 1970.

Lastrucci, C. "Looking Forward: A Case for Hard-Nosed Methodology." *American Sociologist*, 1970, *6*, 273–275.

Law, J. "Theories and Methods in the Sociology of Science: An Interpretive Approach." *Social Science Information*, 1974, *13* (4/5), 163–172.

Lazarsfeld, P. F. "Historical Background." Pittsburgh: Department of Sociology, University of Pittsburgh, 1975.

Leik, R. K. "Casual Models with Nominal and Ordinal Data: Retrospective." In D. R. Heise (Ed.), *Sociological Methodology 1977*. San Francisco: Jossey-Bass, 1976.

Levine, M. "Scientific Method and the Advisory Model: Some Preliminary Thoughts." *American Psychologist*, 1974, *29*, 661–677.

Levinsohn, F. H. "Letter to the Editor." *American Sociologist*, 1976, *11*, 175–178.

Lewis, H. "A Program Responsive to New Knowledge and Values." In E. J. Mullen, J. R. Dumpson, and Associates (Eds.), *Evaluation of Social Intervention*. San Francisco: Jossey-Bass, 1972.

Library of Congress. *The National Union Catalog, 1963–67*. Vols. 1–59. Ann Arbor, Mich.: Edwards, 1969.

Library of Congress. *The National Union Catalog, 1968–72*. Vols. 1–104. Ann Arbor, Mich.: Edwards, 1973.

Library of Congress. *The National Union Catalog, 1973*. Vols. 1–16. Washington, D.C.: Library of Congress, 1974.

Library of Congress. *The National Union Catalog, 1974*. Vols. 1–8. Washington, D.C.: Library of Congress, 1975.

Lightfield, E. T. "Output and Recognition of Sociologists." *American Sociologist*, 1971, *6*, 128–133.

Lin, N., and Nelson, C. E. "Bibliographic Reference Patterns in Core Sociological Journals, 1965–1966." *American Sociologist*, 1969, *4*, 47–50.

Lindsey, D. "Distinction, Achievement, and Editorial Board

Membership." *American Psychologist*, 1976, *31*, 799–804.

Lindsey, D. "Participation and Influence in Publication Review Proceedings: A Reply." *American Psychologist*, 1977a, *32* (7), 579–586.

Lindsey, D. "The Processing of Self-Criticism by Social Work Journals." *American Psychologist*, 1977b, *32* (7), 1110–1115.

Lindsey, D. "The Operations of Professional Journals in Social Work." *Journal of Sociology and Social Welfare*, 1978, *5*, 273–298.

Lindsey, D. "The Corrected Quality Ratio: A Composite Index of Scientific Contribution to Knowledge." *Social Studies of Science*, in press.

Lindsey, D., and Lindsey, T. W. "The Outlook of Journal Editors and Referees on the Normative Criteria of Scientific Craftsmanship: Viewpoints from Psychology, Social Work, and Sociology." *Quality and Quantity: European-American Journal of Methodology*, 1977, *12*, 45–62.

Lindsey, D., and Staulcup, H. "Improving Measures of Scientific Contributions to Knowledge." Paper presented at the annual meeting of the American Sociological Association, Chicago, September 1977.

Line, M. B., Sandison, A., and McGregor, J. *Patterns of Citations to Articles Within Journals: A Preliminary Test of Scatter, Concentration and Obsolescence.* Bath, England: Bath University Library, 1972.

Lissitz, R. W. "A Longitudinal Study of the Research Methodology in the *Journal of Abnormal and Social Psychology*, the *Journal of Nervous and Mental Disease*, and the *American Journal of Psychiatry*." *Journal of the History of the Behavioral Sciences*, 1969, *5*, 248–255.

Lodahl, J. B., and Gordon, G. "The Structure of Scientific Fields and the Functioning of University Graduate Departments." *American Sociological Review*, 1972, *37*, 57–72.

Loeb, M. B. "The Backdrop for Social Research: Theory Making and Model Building." In Leonard Kogan (Ed.), *Social Science Theory and Social Work Research.* New York: National Association of Social Workers, 1960.

Lowry, D. H., and others. "Protein Measurement with the Folin

Phenol Reagent." *Journal of Biological Chemistry*, 1951, *193*, 256-265.

Lynn, R. S. *Knowledge for What?* Boston: Grove Press, 1964. (Originally published 1938).

Lyons, M. "Techniques for Using Ordinal Measures in Regression and Path Analysis." In H. L. Costner (Ed.), *Sociological Methodology 1971*. San Francisco: Jossey-Bass, 1971.

McCartney, J. "Confronting the Journal Publication Crisis: A Proposal for a Council of Social Science Journal Editors." *American Sociologist*, 1976, *11*, 144-152.

McCartney, J. L. "Making Sense of Reviewers' Comments." Paper presented at the Southern Sociological Association meeting, New Orleans, March 1978.

Mace, K. C., and Warner, H. D. "Ratings of Psychology Journals." *American Psychologist*, 1973, *28*, 184-186.

MacRae, D., Jr. "Growth and Decay Curves in Scientific Citations." *American Sociological Review*, 1969, *34*, 631-635.

MacRae, D., Jr. *The Social Functions of Social Science*. New Haven, Conn.: Yale University Press, 1976.

McReynolds, P. "Reliability of Ratings of Research Papers." *American Psychologist*, 1971, *25*, 400-401.

Mahoney, M. J. *The Scientist as Subject*. Cambridge, Mass.: Ballinger, 1976.

Mahoney, M. J. "Publication Prejudices: An Experimental Study of Confirmatory Bias in the Peer Review System." *Cognitive Therapy and Research*, 1977, *1*, 161-175.

Mahoney, M. J. "Publish or Perish." *Human Behavior*, 1978, *2*, 38-41.

Mahoney, M. J., Kazdin, A. E., and Kenigsberg, M. "Getting Published." *Cognitive Therapy and Research*, 1978, *2*, 69-70.

Manis, J. G. "Some Academic Influences Upon Publication Productivity." *Social Forces*, 1951, *29*, 267-272.

Maslow, A. H. *The Psychology of Science*. New York: Harper & Row, 1966.

Meile, R. L. "The Case Against Double Jeopardy." *American Sociologist*, 1977, *12*, 52.

Menard, H. W. *Science: Growth and Change*. Cambridge, Mass.: Harvard University Press, 1971.

Merton, R. K. *Social Theory and Social Structure*. New York: Free Press, 1957.

Merton, R. K. *The Sociology of Science: Theoretical and Empirical Investigations*. Chicago: University of Chicago Press, 1973.

Merton, R. K. *Sociological Ambivalence*. New York: Free Press, 1977.

Meyers, L. "On the Reliability of the Ratings." *Television Quarterly,* 1962, *1*, 50–63.

Mills, C. W. *The Sociological Imagination*. New York: Oxford University Press, 1959.

Mitroff, I. I. *The Subjective Side of Science*. Amsterdam: Elsevier, 1974.

Mitroff, I. I., and Chubin, D. E. "Peer Review: A Dialectical Policy Analysis." Unpublished paper, Department of Sociology, University of Pennsylvania, 1978.

Moore, W. J. "The Relative Quality of Economic Journals: A Suggested Rating System." *Western Economic Journal*, 1972, *10*, 156–169.

Moravcsik, M. J., and Murugesan, P. "Some Results on the Function and Quality of Citations." *Social Studies of Science*, 1975, *5*, 86–92.

Mosteller, F., and Tukey, J. W. *Data Analysis and Regression*. Reading, Mass.: Addison-Wesley, 1977.

Mulaik, S. A. *The Foundations of Factor Analysis*. New York: McGraw-Hill, 1972.

Mulkay, M. J. "Norms and Ideology in Science." *Social Science Information*, 1976, *15*, 637–656.

Mullins, N. C. "The Development of Specialties in Social Science: The Case of Ethnomethodology." *Science Studies*, 1973, *3*, 245–273.

Mullins, N. C. "New Causal Theory: An Elite Specialty in Social Sciences." *History of Political Economy*, 1975, *7*, 499–529.

Myers, C. R. "Journal Citations and Scientific Eminence in Contemporary Psychology." *American Psychologist*, 1970, *25*, 1041–1048.

Narin, F., Pinski, G., and Gee, H. H. "Structure of the Biomedical Literature." *Journal of the American Society for*

Information Science, 1976, *27*, 25–45.

National Academy of Sciences. *Social and Behavioral Science Programs in the National Science Foundation*. Washington, D.C.: National Academy of Sciences, National Research Council, 1976.

National Association of Social Workers. *Abstracts for Social Workers*. Vols. 1–10. New York: National Association for Social Workers, 1965–1974.

National Science Foundation. *Graduate Student Support and Manpower Resources in Graduate Science Education, Fall 1970*. Series 71-27. Washington, D.C.: National Science Foundation, 1971.

National Science Foundation. "Editorial Processing Centers: Feasibility and Promise." Report C-769. Washington, D.C.: National Science Foundation, 1975.

Nielsen, A. C. *What Do the Ratings Really Say?* Chicago: A. C. Nielsen, 1964.

Nisbett, R. E., and Wilson, T. D. "The Halo Effect: Evidence for Unconscious Alterations of Judgments." *Journal of Personality and Social Psychology*, 1977, *35*, 250–256.

Orlov, A. "On the Small Prank." *American Sociologist*, 1973, *8*, 195.

Orlov, A. "Demythologizing Scholarly Publishing." In P. G. Altbach and S. McVey (Eds.), *Perspectives on Publishing*. Lexington, Mass.: Heath, 1976.

Ornstein, M. *The Role of Scientific Societies in the Seventeenth Century*. Chicago: University of Chicago Press, 1938.

Oromaner, M. "Collaboration and Impact: The Career of Multi-authored Publications." *Social Science Information*, 1974a, *14*, 147–155.

Oromaner, M. "The Impact of Sponsored and Non-Sponsored Publication in Sociology." *American Sociologist*, 1974b, *9*, 36–39.

Osgood, C. E., Suci, G. J., and Tannenbaum, P. H. *The Measurement of Meaning*. Urbana: University of Illinois Press, 1957.

Overall, J., and Klett, C. J. *Applied Multivariate Analysis*. New York: McGraw-Hill, 1972.

Parsons, T. *The Social System*. New York: Free Press, 1951.

Parsons, T. *Essays in Sociological Theory.* (rev. ed.) New York: Free Press, 1954.

Patel, N. "Quantitative and Collaborative Trends in American Sociological Research." *American Sociologist,* 1972, 7, 5-6.

Pearson, G. *The Deviant Imagination: Psychiatry, Social Work and Social Change.* New York: Holmes & Meier, 1975.

Peters, C. "Multiple Submissions: Why Not?" *American Sociologist,* 1976, *11,* 165-179.

Peterson, D. J. "Is Psychology a Profession?" *American Psychologist,* 1976, *31,* 572-581.

Pfeffer, J., Leong, A., and Strehl, K. "Paradigm Development and Particularism: Journal Publication in Three Scientific Disciplines." *Social Forces,* 1977, *55,* 938-951.

Pfeffer, J., Salancik, G. R., and Leblebici, H. "The Effects of Uncertainty on the Use of Social Influence in Organizational Decision Making." *Administrative Science Quarterly,* 1976, *21,* 227-245.

Polanyi, M. *Personal Knowledge.* Chicago: University of Chicago Press, 1958.

Poole, R. *Toward Deep Subjectivity.* Middlesex, England: Penguin Books, 1972.

Popper, K. *Conjectures and Reflections.* London: Routledge & Kegan Paul, 1963.

Porter, A. L. "Use Lists with Caution." *American Psychologist,* 1976, *31,* 674-675.

Porter, J. R. "Challenges to Editors of Scientific Journals." *Science,* 1963, *141,* 1014-1017.

Powell, W. W. "Publishers' Decision Making: What Criteria Do They Use in Deciding Which Books to Publish?" *Social Research,* in press.

Prescott, S., and Csikszentmihalyi, M. "Institutional Status and Publication Rates in Professional Journals." Paper presented at annual meeting of the American Sociological Association, Chicago, September 1977.

Price, D. J. *Science Since Babylon.* New Haven, Conn.: Yale University Press, 1961.

Price, D. J. *Little Science, Big Science.* New York: Columbia University Press, 1963.

Price, D. J. "Networks of Scientific Papers." *Science*, 1965, *149*, 510-515.

Price, D. J. "Communication in Science: The Ends—Philosophy and Forecast." In A. de Reuch and J. Knight (Eds.), *Ciba Foundation Symposium on Communication in Science: Documentation and Automation*. London: Churchill, 1967.

Price, D. J. "The Structures of Publication in Science and Technology." In W. H. Greiber and D. R. Marquis (Eds.), *Factors in the Transfer of Technology*. Cambridge, Mass.: M.I.T. Press, 1969.

Price, D. J. "Citation Measures of Hard Science, Soft Science, Technology, and Nonscience." In C. E. Nelson and D. K. Pollock (Eds.), *Communication Among Scientists and Engineers*. Lexington, Mass.: Heath, 1970.

Price, D. J. "The Productivity of Research Scientists." In *Yearbook of Science and the Future 1975*. Chicago: Encyclopaedia Britannica, 1974.

Quandt, R. E. "Some Quantitative Aspects of the Economics Journal Literature." *Journal of Political Economy*, 1976, *84*, 741-755.

Ravetz, J. R. *Scientific Knowledge and Its Social Problems*. London: Oxford University Press, 1971.

Reskin, B. F. "Sex Differences in Status Attainment in Science: The Case of the Postdoctoral Fellowship." *American Sociological Review*, 1976, *41*, 597-612.

Reskin, B. F. "Scientific Productivity and the Reward Structure of Science." *American Sociological Review*, 1977, *42*, 491-504.

Rhodes, L. J. *The Author's Guide to Selected Journals*. Washington, D.C.: American Sociological Association, 1974.

Ringle, J. "Review of Reports for Science." *AAAS Bulletin*, March 1969.

Roche, T., and Smith, D. L. "Use of the Citation to Evaluate Journals, Departments, and Individuals: A Study in the Stratification of Sociology." Paper presented at the annual American Sociological Association meeting, New York, September 1976.

Rodman, H. "The Moral Responsibility of Journal Editors and

Referees." *American Sociologist*, 1970, *5*, 351–357.

Rodman, H., and Mancini, J. A. "Editors, Manuscripts, and Equal Treatment." *Research in Higher Education*, 1977, *7*, 369–374.

Roose, K. D., and Andersen, C. J. *A Rating of Graduate Programs*. Washington, D.C.: American Council on Education, 1970.

Rosen, A. "Doctoral Education, Professional Culture, and Development of Social Work Knowledge." *Applied Social Studies*, 1969, *1*, 151–159.

Rosenberg, M. *The Logic of Survey Analysis*. New York: Basic Books, 1968.

Rosenblatt, A. "The Practitioner's Use and Evaluation of Research." *Social Work*, 1968, *13*, 53–59.

Rosenthal, D. *Genetic Theory and Abnormal Behavior*. New York: McGraw-Hill, 1970.

Ross, L. "The Intuitive Psychologist and His Shortcomings: Distortions in the Attribution Process." *Advances in Experimental Social Psychology*, 1977, *10*, 173–200.

Ross, L., Lepper, M. R., and Hubbard, M. "Perseverance in Self-Perception and Social Perception: Biased Attributional Processes in the Debriefing Paradigm." *Journal of Personality and Social Psychology*, 1975, *32*, 880–892.

Rothman, R. A. "A Dissenting View on the Scientific Ethos." *British Journal of Sociology*, 1972, *23*, 102–108.

Rudd, E. "The Effect of Alphabetic Order of Author Listing on the Careers of Scientists." *Social Studies of Science*, 1977, *7*, 268–269.

Sarbin, T. R. "Schizophrenia is a Myth, Born of Metaphor, Meaningless." *Psychology Today*, 1972, *6*, 18–27.

Schaeffer, D. L. "Do APA Journals Play Professional Favorites?" *American Psychologist*, 1970, *25*, 362–365.

Scheff, T. J. *Being Mentally Ill*. Chicago: Aldine, 1966.

Schwartz, B. *Queuing and Waiting: Studies in the Social Organization of Access and Delay*. Chicago: University of Chicago Press, 1975.

Scott, W. A. "Interreferee Agreement on Some Characteristics of Manuscripts Submitted to the *Journal of Personality and*

Social Psychology." *American Psychologist*, 1974, *29*(9), 689–702.

Scribner, R. A., and Chalk, R. A. (Eds.). "Adapting Science to Social Needs." Report No. 76-R-8. Washington, D.C.: American Association for the Advancement of Science, 1977.

Shaw, B. T. "The Use of Quality and Quantity of Publication as Criteria for Evaluating Scientists." Agriculture Research Service, USDA Miscellaneous Publication No. 1041. Washington, D.C.: U.S. Department of Agriculture, 1967.

Siegal, S. *Non-Parametric Statistics for the Behavioral Sciences.* New York: McGraw-Hill, 1956.

Silverman, R. J. "The Education Editor as Futurist." *Teachers College Record*, 1976, *77*, 473–493.

Simon, J. L. "A Plan to Improve the Attribution of Scholarly Articles." *American Sociologist*, 1970, *5*, 264–267.

Smigel, E., and Ross, H. L. "Factors in the Editorial Decision." *American Sociologist*, 1970, *5*, 19–21.

Smith, R. B. *Continuities in Ordinal Path Analysis.* Santa Barbara: Department of Sociology, University of California, 1974.

Sociological Abstracts, Inc. *Sociological Abstracts.* Vols. 1–22. San Diego, Calif.: Sociological Abstracts, 1953–1974.

Spencer, N. J., Mahoney, J., and Hartnett, J. "Journal Editors and the Charge of Unfair Reviewing." Paper presented at the Southeast Psychological Association meeting in Atlanta, March 16, 1978.

Spiegel-Rosing, I., and Price, D. (Eds.). *Science, Technology, and Society.* Beverly Hills, Calif.: Sage, 1977.

Stinchcombe, A. "Letter to the Editor." *American Sociologist*, 1976, *11*, 170–172.

Stinchcombe, A. L., and Ofshe, R. "On Journal Editing as a Probabilistic Process." *American Sociologist*, 1969, *4*, 116–117.

Toffler, A. *Future Shock.* New York: Random House, 1970.

Tuckman, H. P. *Publication, Teaching, and the Academic Reward Structure.* Lexington, Mass.: Heath, 1976.

Tukey, J. W. "Keeping Research in Contact with the Literature: Citation Indices and Beyond." *Journal of Chemical Documents*, 1962, *2*, 34.

Turk, A. "Letter to the Editor." *American Sociologist*, 1976, *11*, 169-170.

Turner, R. "Letter to the Editor." *American Sociologist*, 1976, *11*, 168-169.

Ulrich's International Periodical Directory. (15th ed.) New York: Bowker, 1973.

Upper, D. "The Unsuccessful Self-Treatment of a Case of Writer's Block." *Journal of Applied Behavior Analysis*, 1974, 7, 497.

Van Dyne, L. " 'Spreading Chaos' Seen in Scholarly Publishing." *Chronicle of Higher Education*, 1975, *10*, 11.

Wanderer, J. "Academic Origins of Contributors to the American Sociological Review, 1955-1965." *American Sociologist* 1966, *1*, 241-243.

Ward, A. W., Hall, B. W., and Schram, C. F. "Evaluation of Published Educational Research—National Survey." *American Educational Research Journal*, 1975, *12*, 109-128.

Weed, P., and Greenwald, S. "The Myth of Statistics." *Social Work*, 1973, *18* (2), 113-115.

Weinberger, R., and Tripodi, T. "Trends in Types of Research Reported in Selected Social Work Journals, 1956-65." *Social Service Review*, 1969, *43*, 439-447.

Whitley, R. "The Formal Communications System of Science: A Study of the Organization of British Social Science Journals." *Sociological Review*, 1970a, *16*, 163-179.

Whitley, R. "The Operation of Science Journals: Two Case Studies in British Social Science." *Sociological Review*, 1970b, *18* (2), 241-258.

Wiener, J. "The Footnote Fetish." *Telos*, 1977, *31*, 172-177.

Wilson, T. P. "On Interpreting Ordinal Analogies to Multiple-Regression and Path Analysis." *Social Forces*, 1974, *53*, 196-199.

Winer, B. J. *Statistical Principles in Experimental Design*. New York: McGraw-Hill, 1962.

Wolff, W. M. "A Study of Criteria for Journal Manuscripts." *American Psychologist*, 1970, *25*, 636-639.

Wolff, W. M. "Publication Problems in Psychology and an Explicit Evaluation Scheme for Manuscripts." *American Psychologist*, 1973, *28* (3), 257-261.

Xerox University Microfilms. *Comprehensive Dissertation Index, 1861-1971.* Ann Arbor, Mich.: Xerox University Microfilms, 1973.

Yoels, W. C. "Destiny or Dynasty: Doctoral Origins and Appointment Patterns of Editors of the *American Sociological Review*, 1948-1968." *American Sociologist*, 1971, *6*, 134-139.

Yoels, W. C. "The Structure of Scientific Fields and the Allocation of Editorships on Scientific Journals: Some Observations on the Politics of Knowledge." *Sociological Quarterly*, 1974, *15*, 264-276.

Zuckerman, H. A. "Patterns of Name Ordering Among Authors of Scientific Papers: A Study of Symbolism and Its Ambiguity." *American Journal of Sociology*, 1968, *74*, 276-291.

Zuckerman, H. A. "Stratification in American Science." *Sociological Inquiry*, 1970, *40*, 235-257.

Zuckerman, H. A. *The Scientific Elite*. New York: Free Press, 1977.

Zuckerman, H. A., and Merton, R. K. "Patterns of Evaluation in Science: Institutionalism, Structure, and Functions of the Referee System." *Minerva*, 1971, *9* (1), 66-100.

Index